Johann Georg Zimmermann, Hugh Sempill

Doctor Zimmermann's Conversations with the late King of Prussia

Johann Georg Zimmermann, Hugh Sempill

Doctor Zimmermann's Conversations with the late King of Prussia

ISBN/EAN: 9783337297510

Printed in Europe, USA, Canada, Australia, Japan

Cover: Foto ©Suzi / pixelio.de

More available books at **www.hansebooks.com**

DOCTOR ZIMMERMANN's

CONVERSATIONS

WITH THE LATE

KING OF PRUSSIA,

WHEN HE ATTENDED HIM IN HIS LAST ILLNESS
A LITTLE BEFORE HIS DEATH.

TO WHICH ARE ADDED,

SEVERAL CURIOUS PARTICULARS AND ANECDOTES
OF THAT EXTRAORDINARY PRINCE.

TRANSLATED FROM THE LAST EDITION.

LONDON:
PRINTED FOR C. FORSTER, No. 41, POULTRY.
MDCCXCI.

Dr. ZIMMERMANN'S CONVERSATIONS WITH THE KING OF PRUSSIA.

FREDERIC THE GREAT had been for ſome time declared incurable by very able phyſicians; the greater part of his ſubjects conſidered him as literally dead; all Europe judged his ſituation ſuch as to preclude every hope of relief; the courtiers of Berlin had even purchaſed their mourning; and the expectation of his approaching end had cauſed many caſtles to be built in the air, and given activity to the imagination of many ſpeculating heads, when, on the 9th of June 1786, I received the following letter from his majeſty.

" DR. ZIMMERMANN,

" FOR eight months paſt I have been violently afflicted with an aſthma. The phyſicians of this country give me medicines of every kind; but, inſtead of affording me relief, they tend only to render my diſorder worſe. As the reputation of your ſkill is well known throughout all the northern parts of Europe, I ſhould be very glad if you would take a jaunt hither, for a fortnight, that I may conſult you reſpecting my health, and the circumſtances of my preſent caſe.—You may readily believe that I will defray the expences of your journey, and make you a proper compenſation for your trouble:—if you agree, therefore, to this propoſal, I ſhall ſend you a letter to his royal highneſs the duke of York, who will readily grant you permiſſion to comply with my requeſt: and, in this hope, I beg that God may take you under his ſacred and ſafe protection.

" *Potſdam, June* 6, 1786."

Though alarmed, at firſt, by the contents of this letter, I ſoon aſſumed courage after I had made the following reflections: " I am undoubtedly indebted to Providence," ſaid I, " for this mark of his majeſty's confidence; " and,

" and, under the divine direction, one may " walk with a firm ſtep, and with perfect ſafety, " in the moſt dangerous paths. Frederic, it is " true, never had much faith either in phy- " ſicians or medicine; and as he has always " treated our art as quackery, he will be more " tenacious of the opinion he has formed, that " no relief can be given him. He is, and muſt " be, incurable, ſince phyſicians ſo ſkilful as " thoſe who have hitherto attended him, have " not been able to free him from his malady. " However, it muſt be intereſting, and inſtruc- " tive, to have a near view of ſo extraordinary " a man; and to converſe with him in his laſt " moments. How often does it happen, that " I can ſay nothing elſe at the cloſe of the day, " but that I have aſcended, and deſcended, ſo " many pairs of ſtairs! Will it not be better " to brave every danger that may threaten me " at *Sans-Souci*, than to be always leading ſo " inſipid and monotonous a life? Even ſup- " poſing that the king's incredulity, with regard " to phyſicians, is invincible, as I doubt not it " is, I have, however, great faith in Frederic. " As a phyſician, he may eſteem me very little, " and treat me with contempt; but as a man, " I am certain, he will not deſpiſe me: for with " him, people of worth and good ſenſe have

" always preserved their rights. Besides, I " have learned by long experience that it is " much easier to live with great men, than men " of ordinary rank. There is no occasion, there- " fore, to be afraid of having intercourse with " the king, however peevish or morose he may " be. I know also, that some of the most dis- " tinguished princes generally display benevo- " lence and goodness of heart upon many occa- " sions, notwithstanding all the reasons which they " may have for despising mankind in general."

By reflections such as these I overcame all my uneasiness, and roused my courage so far, as to resolve to pay this *terrible visit* at *Sans-Souci*. I told no person that I had received a letter from his Prussian majesty; because at this time all the gazettes announced that he was better; that he rode out on horseback; and that the summer seemed to have revived him. No one would have believed this intelligence, had it been known that I was called to *Sans-Souci*. Having determined to go thither, I wrote to his majesty as follows:

" SIRE,

" I SHOULD think myself the happiest of " men, if my presence should prove useful to " your majesty. For forty years past, I have " followed you with the same interest, and the

" same

" ſame zeal, as that with which I am about to " depart for Potſdam.

" The duke of York, had he known that " your majeſty had done me the honour to write " to me, would have made me ſet out imme- " diately: but I thought it my duty to con- " form to your majeſty's orders, ſince you have " thought proper to wait for my anſwer be- " fore you ſend a letter to the duke.

" Could wiſhing make one a good phyſician, " I am convinced that your majeſty would be " cured the moment I had the honour of ſeeing " you.

" To that moment I look forward with ea- " gerneſs, enthuſiaſm, and courage."

I waited with the utmoſt impatience for the king's anſwer; but as it had not arrived on the 16th of June, I thought it neceſſary to communicate my ſecret to the duke of York, begging him to make it known to the miniſters of his Britiſh majeſty, without whoſe conſent I could not be abſent from Hanover. Four days after, I received the following anſwer, which induced me to ſet out immediately for Potſdam.

" Dr. Zimmermann,

" I WAS extremely happy to learn by your " letter, of the 10th inſtant, which I have re-

" ceived, that you intend to come and ſtay a
" few days with me. I expect you, therefore,
" and have ſent, along with this, a letter for the
" duke of York, of which I ſpoke to you be-
" fore, and which you will be ſo kind as deliver
" to him, in my name; and may God take
" you under his holy and ſafe protection.

" *Potſdam, June* 16, 1786."

Having paſſed privately through Brunſwick, Magdeburg, and Brandenburg, under the title of a Ruſſian merchant, I arrived at Potſdam on the night of the 23d. At the gate, I told my name to the officer on guard; but when he aſked me, according to cuſtom, whether I had come to that city on my own private affairs, or in a public capacity, I told him that I viſited Potſdam merely as a traveller, in order to ſhew it to my ſpouſe.

A little before midnight, the door of my apartment, at the inn where I lodged, was ſuddenly opened by a young officer belonging to the firſt battalion of guards, who aſked me, in a very military tone, *if I was there by the king's order*. This queſtion of the lieutenant I thought rather ſingular: "Sir," ſaid I, "do you aſk "that queſtion in the name of the king?" *Yes*, replied he—*Yes*, ſaid I alſo; and immediately the

the door was ſhut, a little more gently than it had been opened.

The king, who had ordered information to be brought to him, the moment I arrived, was made acquainted, next morning at four o'clock, with the anſwers, word for word, which I had given at the gate of the city, and at the inn. This circumſtance afforded me great pleaſure, as it enabled his majeſty to judge of my diſcretion, from what I had ſaid to his officers. I had afterwards ſeveral opportunities of giving him freſh proofs of my prudence in this reſpect, with which he appeared to be extremely well ſatisfied.

June the 24th was the firſt, and the moſt terrible of all thoſe days which I paſſed with his majeſty. I may venture to ſay, that it was one of the moſt painful and diſagreeable I ever experienced. None of thoſe which I afterwards ſpent with Frederic had the leaſt reſemblance to it: they all flowed on peaceably and without the leaſt uneaſineſs.

At ſix in the morning, his majeſty ſent to tell me, that he was informed of my arrival at Potſdam, and that he wiſhed to ſee me in two hours. With ſome emotion, though cool and collected, I repaired, at half after ſeven, to *Sans-Souci:* but when I came to the gate of

Brandenburg, near the Egyptian obelifk, which ftands on a fmall mount, I could not help imploring the Divine affiftance: no one, perhaps, ever prayed with fo much fervour upon that eminence. When I reached the habitation of the greateft of kings, I found myfelf furrounded by the moft auguft tranquillity, and I perceived nothing, far or near, but calmnefs and folitude. An officer of the king's houfehold, a perfon with whom I was not acquainted, conducted me to the office of the private fecretaries, to which the cabinet counfellors are accuftomed to go every morning at day-break; and there he defired me to wait for his majefty's *valet de chambre*, who would introduce me to him.

Whilft I was waiting, he remained with me, and we began a very fingular converfation. He told me, that he was requefted by feveral people of Berlin, who wifhed to confult me, to afk how long I would remain at Potfdam, and if I would come to the former city. He told me alfo, that he had in his pocket a poem, written by madam Karchin, on my arrival at Potfdam.

I could not, undoubtedly, have obferved greater fecrecy on any bufinefs than I did, both at Hanover, and on the road, refpecting that which had called me to Potfdam. "How then," faid I to myfelf, "can it be poffible, that

"madam

" madam Karchin has already written a poem " on my arrival?" My conductor, however, informed me that all Berlin had known ſome weeks before of the king's having invited me to ſee him; and that, as I had not come ſooner, it had been ſpread abroad, that I had written that I was at Pyrmont, and could not comply with his wiſhes. All this aſtoniſhed me ſo much the more, as I conſidered myſelf, at *Sans-Souci*, to be in the moſt ſecret place in the world. The whole matter was at length cleared up, in the moſt natural manner; for the news of the king having ſent for me had paſſed through that channel by which every thing in the world is conveyed. A lady of very diſtinguiſhed rank, ſiſter to a nobleman who had an opportunity of knowing that his majeſty had wrote to me, learned this intelligence under the ſeal of ſecrecy, and had, in the ſame manner, entruſted it to the whole city of Berlin.—" But tell me, " ſir," ſaid I, " if you pleaſe, how the king is, " and who is his phyſician?"—" The king," replied he, " is very ill; and, at preſent, one " of his huſſars in waiting is his phyſician." " One of his huſſars in waiting his phyſician!" added I. " Yes, ſir," continued he; " and " ſometimes his majeſty is his own phyſician. " This huſſar is his principal valet de chambre;

" his

" his name is Schoening.—Stop; here he comes " to conduct you to the king."

Mr. Schoening saluted me very politely, but in a grave manner, and with much reserve. Concluding, very justly, that next to his majesty it was of some importance to be on a good footing with him, after I had recovered myself a little, I did and said every thing that my knowledge and the experience I had acquired of mankind, during the course of my life, could dictate, in order to gain over this hussar.

I found Mr. Schoening to be a sensible, prudent man, who spoke well, with much shrewdness and freedom; and who appeared to be perfectly acquainted with Frederic. He did not conceal from me, that he was an intimate friend of professor Selle, the physician whom the king had dismissed a little before. This confession greatly increased the good opinion I had already formed of him; because such frankness is not usual among courtiers. However, as it could not be very agreeable to him to see a stranger called in to attend his majesty, in the room of his friend, I thought it necessary to be very cautious in my conversation with him. Having followed Mr. Schoening as far as the last anti-chamber, I saw there, above a commode, two very large portraits of the emperor

Joſeph II. which I had remarked in 1771. The remembrance of thoſe ſenſations which I experienced when I aſcended the little hill, and of the reflections that then occurred to me, diſſipated all my fears; and in this ſituation of mind I entered the apartment of the king, whom I found ſitting in a large elbow chair, with his back turned towards that ſide of the room by which I had entered. He had on his head a large hat, very much worn, ornamented with a plume of feathers equally ancient; and his dreſs conſiſted of a ſurtout, of ſky blue ſatin, all bedaubed, and tinged of a browniſh yellow colour before, with Spaniſh ſnuff. He wore boots; and reſted one of his legs, which was very much ſwelled, upon a ſtool; while the other hung down to the floor. When he perceived me, he pulled off his hat, in a very polite and affable manner; and in a mild tone of voice ſaid, "I return you many thanks, ſir, "for your kindneſs in coming hither, and for "the ſpeed with which you have performed "your journey." I was perfectly ſenſible that my journey had not been performed with very great diſpatch; but, reflecting that his majeſty could not be ignorant that, in the dry ſeaſon, one muſt be ſtopped every moment in the ſands of Brandenburg, and that poſt horſes are

wretched

wretched animals, I did not think it neceſſary to make any apology for my delay. "The duke "of York," ſaid I, "requeſted me to deliver "this letter to your majeſty."

Frederic read the letter, and our converſation began in the following manner:

FREDERIC.

I am much obliged to the duke of York, for permitting you to come hither.

ZIMMERMANN.

The duke of York wiſhes, as ardently as I do, that my journey may be ſerviceable to your majeſty.

FREDERIC.

How does the duke of York do?

ZIMMERMANN.

Very well—He is always active, lively, and full of ſpirits.

FREDERIC.

I love the duke of York as tenderly as a father can love a ſon.

ZIMMERMANN.

The duke of York is fully ſenſible of the value of the good opinion which your majeſty entertains of him.

FREDERIC.

You ſee I am very ill.

ZIMMER-

ZIMMERMANN.

Your majeſty's eye is as good as when I had the honour of ſeeing you here fifteen years ago. I obſerve not the leaſt diminution in that fire, and vigour, with which your majeſty's eyes were then animated.

FREDERIC.

Oh! I am grown very old, and I find myſelf extremely ill.

ZIMMERMANN.

Germany and Europe are not ſenſible of your majeſty's age and illneſs.

FREDERIC.

My occupations go on in their uſual train.

ZIMMERMANN.

Your majeſty riſes at four in the morning, and by that you prolong and double life.

FREDERIC.

I do not riſe; for I never go to bed—I paſs the whole night in this eaſy chair, in which you now ſee me.

ZIMMERMANN.

Your majeſty wrote to me, that for ſeven months you have found great difficulty in breathing.

FREDERIC.

I am aſthmatic, but not dropſical.—You ſee, however, that my legs are much ſwollen.

ZIMMER-

ZIMMERMANN.

Will your majeſty permit me to examine your legs a little cloſer?

Mr. Schoening being called to pull off his majeſty's boots, I kneeled down, examined his legs, the ſwelling of which extended as far as the thighs—and held my tongue.

FREDERIC.

I have no dropſy.

ZIMMERMANN.

A ſwelling of the legs is often joined with an aſthma. Will your majeſty permit me to feel your lower belly?

FREDERIC.

My belly is big, becauſe I am troubled with flatulencies. There is certainly no water in it.

ZIMMERMANN.

It is indeed diſtended, but it is not hard. May I take the liberty of feeling your majeſty's pulſe?

His pulſe, which was full and ſtrong, indicated a conſiderable degree of fever—He was much oppreſſed, and coughed almoſt without remiſſion.

ZIMMERMANN.

Your pulſe is not weak.

FREDERIC.

It is impoſſible to cure me.

ZIMMERMANN.

But your majeſty may at leaſt be relieved.

FREDERIC.

What would you adviſe me to do?

ZIMMERMANN.

At preſent nothing.—I will go immediately and learn from your *valet de chambre* the whole hiſtory of your diſorder, and read all that your majeſty's phyſicians have written on the ſubject; after which I ſhall have the honour of telling you my ſentiments.

FREDERIC.

That is proper—Schoening knows the whole.

The king then taking off his hat, with much politeneſs, ſaid, "I thank you once more for "your goodneſs in coming hither.—Be ſo kind "as to return to-morrow at three."

Having returned with Mr. Schoening to the private ſecretary's office, without the caſtle, I did not diſcloſe my ſentiments reſpecting the king's diſorder; but I had no reaſon to doubt that his caſe was decidedly dropſical. The ſtate of his breaſt appeared alſo to be very ſuſpicious; not only on account of the oppreſſion, which might be owing to ſome ſeparate cauſe, caufe, and of the water which might be accumulated; but becaufe his majefty's fever and cough made me apprehend an abfcefs. What I told the king, concerning the little change which I obferved in him fince 1771, was true; but that however faid very little. His vifage was not only emaciated and thin, but appeared of that pale yellow colour, which always indicates a depravation of the fluids and folids; and which, in the like cafes, is always a very unfavourable fymptom. His hands were alfo difcoloured and dry; his belly was greatly fwelled; and his legs were not only in the fame condition, as much as legs could be; but the fwelling, as I have already faid, extended even to the thighs.

All the papers concerning the king's ftate were laid before me, by Mr. Schoening. They confifted of a great number of letters, written by profeffor Selle to the huffar who acted as his majefty's *valet de chambre*. This able phyfician kept up a daily correfpondence with him, refpecting the ftate of his majefty's health; but with all the caution and prudence neceffary for fo delicate a tafk.

Mr. Schoening then fhewed me a correfpondence between Mr. Selle, the king's firft phyfician, and Mr. Cothenius, his body phyfician, in

which

which both parties at laſt diſplayed a little warmth. I ſaw, by theſe letters, that Mr. Selle had with great ſagacity obſerved and treated his majeſty's caſe, from firſt to laſt. I learned alſo, that the king had not taken the remedies preſcribed for him, though the beſt that could be adminiſtered, and the moſt ſuitable for his diſorder, above once or twice; and that he was a ſworn enemy to medicines of every kind, except to a digeſtive powder compoſed of rhubarb, Glauber's ſalts, and a few other trifling ingredients, in which alone he had any faith. I learned too that no idea could be formed of the exceſs which the king allowed himſelf in his food; that his cooks were obliged to ſeaſon all his diſhes in ſuch a manner, as was enough to deſtroy his ſtomach; that thoſe which were moſt difficult of digeſtion were his greateſt favourites; that he was paſſionately fond of Pruſſian peas, which are undoubtedly the hardeſt in the world, and would conſequently be conſidered as coarſe even in Lower Saxony and Weſtphalia; that this regimen was the cauſe of thoſe complaints and vomitings which often came upon him after dinner, and of thoſe fits of the colic that attacked him ſeveral times every week; and that nobody durſt venture to remonſtrate with him on this ſubject: that when his phyſicians Selle, Cothenius,

Frefe, and Theden, had prevailed upon him to try any remedies, he would never deviate from his ufual mode of living: that fometimes he would praife a medicine, after he had taken the firft dofe; but after the fecond, when attacked by his qualms, colic, and vomiting, or when he had paffed a bad night, he always blamed the remedy which had been adminiftered to him: that he railed then in a terrible manner againft phyficians and their art; and that, after having harangued the former as the king of Pruffia, he immediately difmiffed them: that after he had fent away his phyficians, he confined himfelf wholly to his regimen, and a few infignificant remedies of his own: that his diforder had by thefe means increafed to fuch a degree; and that it would probably continue the fame to the end.

Such was the account which I received from Mr. Schoening. Every thing that he told me feemed to be ftamped with the feal of truth. Of this I had convincing proofs the fame day, and for fome days following. Though I found little encouragement in Mr. Schoening's relation, yet, on account of the favourable reception which I had met with from his majefty, and the truft I had in Providence, whofe gracious affiftance has, in the courfe of my life,

delivered

delivered me from ſo many dangers, I returned quietly, and contentedly, from *Sans-Souci* to Potſdam, without anticipating in thought what was about to befal me the ſame day. I was to viſit his majeſty at three: at half after twelve, when I was juſt going to ſit down to table, one of the king's chaſſeurs came to tell me, that his majeſty deſired to ſee me as ſoon as I had dined.—Without dining, I immediately ſet out, and hurried as faſt as I could to *Sans-Souci*. In aſcending the little hill before-mentioned, a coach, in which were count Lucheſini and general Goertz, the king's uſual gueſts at table, croſſed the road before me, in its way from the palace. This alarmed me a good deal; because his majeſty, in general, never finiſhed his dinner ſo ſoon. On my arrival, I learned from Mr. Schoening, that, from morning till noon, the king had coughed without interruption; that he had a violent oppreſſion; and that he expectorated a prodigious quantity of blood. On the firſt view, his majeſty's ſituation ſeemed to be highly alarming: he could not ſpeak; coughed very much, and at every fit the blood flowed from his mouth. He could not breathe but after violent and painful efforts. I even thought every moment that my auguſt patient would be ſtifled: ſometimes he could not ſit in his eaſy chair, but was obliged to ſtand up. All his ſtrength ſeemed to be exhauſted, and his head hung down, reſting on his breaſt. Soon after he ſuffered himſelf to drop into his eaſy chair, where he immediately fell aſleep: his face became agitated by convulſive motions; from time to time a rattling noiſe was heard in his throat; and his pulſe was full, quick, and ſtrong, but at the ſame time regular.

I ſtood a long time near him, before he could utter a ſingle ſyllable, and before I could ſpeak to him. Every moment he appeared as if about to be ſuffocated; and the firſt words which he ſaid were, " With all this, I have a violent colic." Scarcely had I returned an anſwer, when he again fell aſleep, and when the rattling in his throat and the convulſive motions returned. A violent fit of coughing ſoon rouſed him from his ſleep, and the blood began to flow from his mouth as before. This melancholy ſcene continued half an hour, when his majeſty found himſelf a little better: I aſked permiſſion to preſcribe ſomething for his relief, which occaſioned the following converſation:

FREDERIC.

What do you intend to do?

ZIMMER-

ZIMMERMANN.

To relieve your breaſt, and ſtop the ſpitting of blood.

FREDERIC.

The ſpitting of blood is nothing; I expectorated fully as much in the war of ſeven years. What muſt I do for my colic?

ZIMMERMANN.

You muſt take a clyſter.

FREDERIC.

It will ſoon go off like a piſtol-ſhot; but, however, I will try your remedy.—What muſt be done beſides?

ZIMMERMANN.

Every thing poſſible muſt be done, to eaſe your breaſt, without irritating the colic. Your majeſty muſt take ſal ammoniac with oxymel.

FREDERIC.

Oxymel is of no ſervice to me. What will the ſal ammoniac do?

ZIMMERMANN.

It will cool and eaſe your breaſt, which is very neceſſary, and will not irritate the colic.

FREDERIC.

Order ſome ſal ammoniac for me; and afterwards tell me if you are at preſent well informed reſpecting my caſe.

ZIMMERMANN.

I am indeed : but I wiſh your majeſty would be pleaſed to allow me to ſend to Berlin for profeſſor Selle, in order that we may concert a plan for the treatment of your diſorder. Selle is better acquainted with your caſe than any one: ſince the beginning of it he has judged well, and always given your majeſty good advice.

With terrible looks, ſparkling eyes, his head raiſed up, and a voice ſuch as I never heard in my life, his majeſty replied, " I expected that plan from you."

ZIMMERMANN.

I will afterwards lay this plan before your majeſty. At preſent I muſt endeavour, as much as poſſible, to relieve the ſymptoms of the moment.

All the king's ſtrength appeared to be exhauſted by this converſation. He ſoon after fell into the ſame ſtate of profound ſleep, his head leaning on his breaſt, and convulſions appeared in his countenance as before.

His majeſty held in one of his hands a white handkerchief, which appeared as if it had been dipped in blood. It was of conſiderable importance to know whether there was not ſome pus mixed with the blood. Seeing, therefore,

a white

a white handkerchief on the table near me, I took it up with one hand, and with the other gently drew towards me that which the king held, when he ſuddenly awoke, raiſed up his head, and darted a furious look at me; but very luckily he ſoon dropped his head again, and fell faſt aſleep. I then put into his hand, with a little more precaution, the handkerchief I had taken from the table; and on examining that which I took in exchange, I found pure blood with a very little phlegm, but no pus at all. The king remained a long time dozing, and always ſeemed to breathe with much difficulty. While he was in that ſtate, the ſal ammoniac was brought; and Frederic having at length awoke, I ſaid, "Here is the ſal ammoniac." He ſhook his head, took the ſalt which I gave him, had a clyſter adminiſtered, and again ſlept for an hour: but the convulſive motions in his face ſtill continued. During theſe painful moments, I was the only perſon with the king, while one or two huſſars attended in the anti-chamber. I conſidered myſelf then as in an aukward ſituation—a ſtranger, and alone with the king of Pruſſia, who appeared to be angry with me on the firſt day of my arrival, before I had time to ſay or do any thing of importance, and fearing every moment to ſee the hero whom the eighteenth century had ſo often dreaded at the head of his armies, and always admired, expire before my eyes, and in my arms. Thoſe who have been in imminent danger, or in alarming agitation of mind, will eaſily comprehend what I ſuffered upon this occaſion.

The day was remarkably warm; the ſweat ran down my face in torrents; and I ſhould certainly, if poſſible, have perſpired blood. Finding myſelf alone with this *awfully great* prince, ſurrounded by the moſt ſolemn tranquillity, I indulged thoughts and reflections which in turns diſtracted me, and inſpired me with courage. Sometimes I fixed my eyes upon the king; ſometimes on a ſuperb buſt of white marble and agate, which ſtood upon the chimney-piece oppoſite to his bed, and which brought to my mind that paſſage of his Epiſtle to Marſhal Keith, where he ſays,

> Virtuous Mark Aurelius,
> An example for mankind,
> My hero, and my model.

Without ſtirring from my place, I obſerved every thing that appeared remarkable in the king, and even in his apartment. With his dreſs, which was a little cynical, he had on his

his left hand two rings, each consisting of a very large single brilliant: on the left he wore another ring less costly, but which was valuable for a different reason; it was a green chrysoprasus from Silesia, which he wore as a memorial of his conquest of that large duchy. Opposite to the door of the king's apartment, which was open, I beheld a beautiful portrait of the emperor Joseph II. It appeared that his majesty had caused it to be put in the above position, that he might never lose sight of so great and enterprising a monarch.

Afterwards recovering myself, and returning to my usual situation, I reflected on the honour I had in being called as a physician to attend the greatest of kings. Thinking on the jealousy which this honour would excite in the minds of those who are vexed to see others accomplish that glorious end to which they are not able to attain, I said to myself, "If they felt all the uneasiness and all the fears which I now experience, I am certain they would be far from envying my condition."

I was not, however, apprehensive of seeing the king expire that day, because he had not the pulse of a dying person, which convinced me that, notwithstanding every unfavourable appearance, the vital strength was not exhausted; and

and becaufe I flattered myfelf that this ftorm might be periodical, and confequently more alarming than dangerous.

Whilft I was abforbed in thefe reflections, his majefty was awaked by another very violent fit of coughing, and a dreadful oppreffion. As foon as he was able to fpeak, he faid, "This fal-ammoniac does not afford me any relief: I will take my digeftive powder." This powder was compofed of cream of tartar, nitre, and crabs eyes. I replied, that it would do very well: it would open and relieve his belly. He then took his digeftive powder; and at the fame time a great quantity of letters were brought to him open, which contained the replies he had given that morning to all the difpatches he had received from foreign countries, and from his own ftates. Thefe letters were laid upon a table, clofe to the fide of his majefty's eafy chair; and, notwithftanding his exhaufted ftate and great weaknefs, he drew them all towards him, and began to read them. I retired fome paces backwards, as far as the door of the anti-chamber, while his majefty read all thefe letters, which were probably very fhort, and with a trembling hand afterwards figned them. When this bufinefs was over, I again advanced before his majefty, who faid a few words to me refpecting his fituation: after which he fell afleep, alternately dozing and coughing; but he expectorated a much fmaller quantity of blood. Being alone above an hour, with Frederic always afleep, I continued my meditations: but however terrible this fcene might be, it ftill exhibited fomething which gave me courage.

"If I can extricate myfelf happily from this painful fituation—if I can obtain," faid I, with a kind of enthufiafm, "the confidence of this terrible prince, I fhall be embarraffed with nothing that may happen to me in the courfe of my life. I fhould not be afraid of prefenting myfelf before all the great men in the world, and of looking them boldly in the face." Sometimes, when the king recollected himfelf, he addreffed a few words to me. He then had fome ftools; the intervals of his being awake were longer; his breathing became freer; and he told me that his colic had left him.

For four hours I was at this fatiguing poft, when his majefty difmiffed me, with thefe words: *Return to-morrow morning at half paft fix.*

June 25th. When I arrived in the king's anti-chamber, at the appointed time, his fecond huffar gave me a thoufand crowns, in in bank-notes, and told me that his majesty wished me to know that this sum was intended to pay the expences of my journey from Hanover to Potsdam; and that I should receive a thousand more for my return.

Having advanced towards the king, he received me very graciously, and with much politeness, and appeared to be in very good humour. "I have slept much better than I expected," said he; "and I find myself quite different from what I was yesterday." He indeed coughed very little, and threw up scarcely any blood; his breast was easier, and his pulse very regular.

When I thanked him for the present I had received, he replied, "The obligation is on my side, for your kindness in coming hither."

We afterwards conversed on the state in which his majesty then found himself. "At present," said I, "it would be best, in my opinion, to continue cooling remedies, and to take care that your belly be kept open." The king appeared to acquiesce, and dismissed me in a very genteel and polite manner, saying, "Be so kind as return after dinner, at three."

I waited upon his majesty according to appointment, and he conversed above half an hour, without saying a single word respecting

his

his ſituation. He was cheerful; in very good humour; from time to time brought up a little blood; and talked, without interruption, of the Engliſh and French literature. A part of our converſation I ſhall mention.

FREDERIC.

Locke and Newton were, of all men, the deepeſt thinkers: but the French underſtand much better than the Engliſh the manner of expreſſing things well.

ZIMMERMANN.

The Engliſh language is, without doubt, very proper for treating of philoſophy, and the higher branches of ſcience: but the parliament always ſees ſome new Demoſthenes ſtart up in its boſom. The Engliſh language is adapted alſo for the ſimple and noble ſtyle of hiſtory; and for works of humour and pleaſantry, it is inferior to no language whatever.

FREDERIC.

Robertſon and Hume are hiſtorians of the firſt claſs; I eſteem them both very much.

ZIMMERMANN.

Gibbon is, perhaps, ſuperior to either of them. All the beauties and dignity that the hiſtorical ſtyle is ſuſceptible of, are united in Gibbon. His periods have an enchanting harmony, and all his thoughts are deep and nervous.

FREDERIC.

What has Gibbon written?

I explained in a few words the contents of Gibbon's work, on the decline and downfall of the Roman empire. The king ſuffered me to go on a long time, without interruption; ſeemed to liſten with much attention and pleaſure; and then took a ſurvey of the German literature.

FREDERIC.

How do the ſciences go on in Hanover?

ZIMMERMANN.

We have ſome men of talents at Hanover, who, without ſhewing it, rouſe a ſpirit of emulation in each other; and this produces ſome intereſting ſparks of genius every year. The Hanoverians are indebted to Gottingen for their knowledge and improvement.

FREDERIC.

Gottingen is much celebrated; but there is not a Hanoverian amongſt its profeſſors.

ZIMMERMANN.

Several of the greateſt men in Germany are ſettled, and teach at Gottingen. There are ſeveral very celebrated profeſſors there, who

are

are Hanoverians by birth: for example, Meiners and Wrisberg.

FREDERIC.

I know Meiners; he wrote a very good book on Swisserland.

ZIMMERMANN.

It is an excellent work, and written with a true attachment to Swisserland, although it has been much condemned in all the thirteen cantons.

We then conversed, for a few minutes, of Swisserland, Haller, and other learned men of that country. The king spoke of Haller with much respect, a proof that he had never read his *Usong*; and afterwards gave his opinion, which was far from being always favourable, of some other literati.

At length his majesty said, with much goodness, "Sir, I wish to see you again to-morrow morning, at eight."

June 26th. The king was still extremely polite, and in the best humour possible. Our conversation was as follows.

FREDERIC.

Have you wrote out the plan according to which my disorder is to be treated?

ZIMMER-

ZIMMERMANN.

No, sire; but I have it in my head; and, if your majesty will permit me, shall have the honour of communicating it to you in a few words.

FREDERIC.

Say whatever you please.

ZIMMERMANN.

Your majesty has many obstructions, especially in the viscera of the lower belly: we must, therefore, endeavour to dissolve all those obstructions, to establish a free circulation of the humours, and to evacuate, as much as possible, all superfluities, without lessening your strength. Your majesty must take nothing at present but a gentle, dissolvent, opening and purgative medicine; afterwards we may administer more active dissolvents and evacuants, and support them by strengthening remedies. This is my whole plan; I know of nothing else.

FREDERIC.

You intend then to cure me?

ZIMMERMANN.

I intend to relieve your majesty, if you will have patience, and allow me the necessary time. A patient relieved is half cured.

FREDE-

FREDERIC.

In that you are right: but what do you intend to give me?

ZIMMERMANN.

A very ſimple, common remedy, known to every body, and uſed formerly by the Greeks and the Romans: the juice of dandelion, boiled to the conſiſtence of honey.

FREDERIC.

I do not know that plant.

ZIMMERMANN.

It may be found in all the meadows in the ſpring.

FREDERIC.

I would gladly know for what *lion* this plant was created.

ZIMMERMANN *(laughing)*.

Pleaſe your majeſty, we ſhall ſee that ſoon.

FREDERIC.

But do you know this plant from your own experience?

ZIMMERMANN.

Yes, from long and frequent experience.

FREDERIC.

I will take that remedy.

His majeſty added, with much good humour, "Adieu, my dear ſir; I will follow all your orders."

Mr. Schœning, who was before the door of the chamber, which was open, and who had heard all our converſation, ſeemed much aſtoniſhed when I went out. " I never," ſaid he, " ſaw the king ſo mild and tractable when medicines were preſcribed for him; and I believe he never in his life behaved with ſo much politeneſs to a phyſician."—At four the ſame day I again viſited the king: he was ſtill very polite and contented, and talked about an hour and a half with me on different ſubjects. Part of our converſation I can relate.

FREDERIC.

Do you often ſee the duke of York? and what is your opinion of him?

ZIMMERMANN.

I ſee the duke of York always when he has occaſion for me; and at any rate generally once a week. He behaves to me with much affability and politeneſs: I am always happy when in his company. His Engliſh education has rendered him very eaſy of acceſs; and he is not acquainted with that haughty ſtiffneſs which is ſo common among the princes of Germany. The duke of York never teaſed and tormented me, as the petty German princes teaſe and torment their phyſicians; his noble ſoul brought no other principles from England to Hanover,

Hanover, than thoſe which are conſiſtent with the rights of mankind: our manners have been new modelled after his; conſequently he has tended greatly to ſoften them, and ſo has that young ſailor prince William Henry. He has baniſhed from Hanover, by his mildneſs and engaging manner, the ariſtocratic reſerve and exceſſive pride of our nobility. It is much to be wiſhed that the ſons of our king would remain among us, in order that they might deſtroy and efface from among our nobles and citizens the ancient Hanoverian manners, half Spaniſh, half German, which they have already much ſoftened.

Having found the duke of York one morning ſick, and aſking permiſſion from him to return in the evening, he replied, "Come if you have nothing of more importance to engage your attention." The duke of York is far from being ſo imperious and proud as many petty cits or gentlemen, who make their footmen ſtyle them My Lord; or as many tradeſmen in Hanover and other cities.

FREDERIC.

I have always known that the people of Hanover had a great deal of the Spaniards in them; and I love the duke of York ſtill more for bringing about this reformation in their manners.

ZIMMERMANN.

Many people of great worth would be highly gratified, did they know how much your majeſty loves the duke of York.

FREDERIC.

I love the duke of York very much. He is highly accompliſhed for his age; poſſeſſes great politeneſs; and diſplays much knowledge. He is, beſides, extremely prudent, and behaves himſelf well. A prince of ſo much merit ought to be greatly eſteemed; for, in general, princes have no merit at all. I have often followed the duke of York in little things, where he could not doubt that I obſerved him.

In thoſe little things, as a man is under no reſtraint, it is much eaſier to ſtudy his diſpoſition than in matters of great importance, where he is on his guard, becauſe he knows that others have their eyes on him. I have always found the duke of York ſuch as I wiſhed to find him.

ZIMMERMANN.

It is impoſſible, ſire, to find any perſon more devoted to your majeſty than the duke of York. He would willingly lay down his life to preſerve yours.

FREDERIC.

FREDERIC.

He knows how much I love him; and I hope in time he will become an able general.

Before he difmiffed me, his majefty promifed that he would next morning take the juice of dandelion which I had prefcribed for him.

June 27th. When I waited upon the king at eight in the morning, the remedy had not been taken; and I found in his majefty no traces of thofe good refolutions which he had formed the day before. That docility, which aftonifhed Mr. Schœning fo much, had entirely difappeared. As foon as I entered the apartment, his majefty played off a battery of arguments againft the juice of dandelion: but I combated them all with the utmoft freedom, which was indeed a tafk of no great difficulty. Our converfation refpecting dandelion continued ftill to grow more animated, and ended in the following manner.

FREDERIC.

I told you before that I would take your medicine but once a day.

ZIMMERMANN.

In that cafe your majefty will have a very large dofe to take at once.

 FREDERIC.

FREDERIC.

How much ?

ZIMMERMANN.

Two or three ſpoonfuls.

FREDERIC.

I do not call that much.

ZIMMERMANN.

So much the better. But two or three ſpoonfuls of the juice of dandelion, taken at once, may occaſion ſickneſs, and even vomiting.

FREDERIC.

In that caſe I will not take the dandelion.

ZIMMERMANN.

What I apprehend perhaps will not happen. Your majeſty may begin by very ſmall doſes.

FREDERIC.

That ſlow method I diſlike.

ZIMMERMANN.

Your majeſty may then take two ſpoonfuls at firſt, with a little fennel water, which is friendly to the ſtomach.

FREDERIC.

May I drink coffee ſoon after ?

ZIMMERMANN.

Half an hour after.

FREDERIC.

FREDERIC.

But is it not poſſible that dandelion may have loſt that virtue which it had in the time of the Greeks and the Romans?

ZIMMERMANN.

I know that plant and its virtues, not from books alone; I have uſed the extract of it for thirty years; every ſpring I adminiſter, perhaps, more than one hundred pounds of it in all diſeaſes ariſing from obſtructions of the viſcera. But, if what I ſay cannot convince or perſuade your majeſty, I beg that, in taking my preſcription of dandelion, you will do with me as Alexander did with his phyſician, who according to report intended to poiſon him. Pleaſe to ſwallow this poiſon in my preſence; let your majeſty then fix your eyes upon me, and you will ſee that I will not change countenance more than the phyſician of the great Alexander.

This pleaſantry ſeemed to make more impreſſion on the king, than all my medical reaſoning: he fell a laughing in the moſt pleaſant and agreeable manner, and ſaid to me, in a reſolute tone, "I will take your preſcription."

He then diſmiſſed me with—"Adieu, my good ſir. You will do me a pleaſure to return after dinner at three, provided it be not inconvenient."

FREDERIC.

(At three o'clock.)—But tell me, is it poſſible that at my age, after all the fatigues I have undergone, and after ſo laborious a life, conſidering my preſent ſufferings, I can hope for the ſmalleſt relief?

ZIMMERMANN.

It is poſſible to relieve you.

FREDERIC.

I cannot believe it.

ZIMMERMANN.

I believe it; becauſe the firſt day, when I waited on your majeſty, you appeared the whole morning ſo weak and exhauſted, that I thought it would be a very long time before you could recover any degree of ſtrength: but when I entered your apartment next morning, trembling with apprehenſion, I found you lively, and in good ſpirits.

FREDERIC.

To morrow morning I will take your dandelion.

June 28th. At ſix o'clock in the morning, his majeſty, before he diſpatched the affairs of government, took two ſpoonfuls of the

juice

juice of dandelion, with fennel water. When I arrived at eight, I learned wonders ſo great, that I could not venture to truſt either my eyes or my ears.

FREDERIC.

Your remedy, my dear Mr. Zimmermann, is a medicinal courier, who, on the firſt orders, repairs with the utmoſt expedition to the place of his deſtination. He poſſeſſes great ſagacity; for he knows where the ſeat of the evil is: you hit the ſpot at which you take aim. You perform miracles; for I am more relieved to-day than I ever was, by all the remedies hitherto given me. In ſhort, I find myſelf better than ever I did during the courſe of my diſorder.

ZIMMERMANN.

I never performed a miracle, nor ever can; and I believe in none but thoſe which your majeſty performed during the war of ſeven years. You beſtow, ſire, too much praiſe on my remedy. You have reſted well laſt night; and you aſcribe to my medicine the relief ariſing from ſleep which has given you that vigour, courage, and confidence, by which you are now animated.

FREDERIC.

No—I am indebted for my relief to your remedy. I have often ſlept well, without finding

ing myſelf better next morning. Obſerve with what facility I breathe.

ZIMMERMANN.

Your majeſty ſpeaks quicker, and with more eaſe.

FREDERIC.

My breaſt has not been ſo free for a long time.

ZIMMERMANN.

Will your majeſty permit me to make one obſervation?

By your perſeverance, you have overcome your enemies; by your conſtancy in all your enterpriſes, you rendered poſſible what was thought impoſſible, and you acquired eternal glory. By the ſame conſtancy you may at preſent alleviate your malady, and all your ſufferings.

FREDERIC.

Will this remedy allay the ſwelling of my legs?

ZIMMERMANN.

Perhaps it will, if it operates by ſtool; but other remedies may do that afterwards.

FREDERIC.

In what time will the dandelion relieve me? ——in two months?

ZIMMERMANN.

In one month perhaps.

After this converſation, the king diſmiſſed me in the moſt cordial manner, and with more ſatisfaction than ever. At three, when I returned, I found him equally contented ; and he diſcourſed with me on different ſubjects.

FREDERIC.

You correſpond with the empreſs of Ruſſia ?

ZIMMERMANN.

The empreſs ſometimes does me the honour to write to me.

FREDERIC.

She conſults you reſpecting her health ?

ZIMMERMANN.

She has not the leaſt occaſion, as ſhe enjoys perfect health.——Literature, humanity, and philoſophy, are the ſubjects of the letters which her majeſty is pleaſed to addreſs to me.

FREDERIC.

It is, however, known every where that the empreſs is ill.

ZIMMERMANN.

The empreſs knows that every body imagines ſo : this often affords her an opportunity of indulging in a little pleaſantry. In one of her letters

letters ſhe told me that her health coſt her fifteen pence a year.

FREDERIC.

The information I have received, on this ſubject, is totally different.

ZIMMERMANN.

Your majeſty knows better than any one how little dependance, in ſuch caſes, is to be placed on information apparently certain. I am fully convinced that what is reported, reſpecting the valetudinary ſtate of the empreſs, cannot be true; for ſhe expoſes herſelf to the greateſt fatigue. Laſt ſummer ſhe accompliſhed a journey of two hundred and fifty German miles, in the higheſt ſpirits, and with the utmoſt compoſure. Good humour never forſakes her; and throughout the whole day her mind is engaged in the moſt active employments. During her moments of relaxation, ſhe lately wrote two codes of laws; one for the Ruſſian nobility, and the other for the cities of her dominions. She has likewiſe undertaken to execute, with her own hand, an aſtoniſhing work, the intention of which is purely philoſophical: this work is a *Comparative Gloſſary* of all the languages, both original and derived, which are ſpoken in the Ruſſian empire. This year ſhe ſent me, as a preſent, ſeveral comedies

medies full of wit and humour, and destined to ridicule superstition, and religious quackery*.

FREDERIC.

I allow that the empress of Russia is a woman of extraordinary genius†.

June 29th. The king was not so well this morning as the day before; but he was no less mild and good-tempered.

FREDERIC.

You understand how to simplify your art; I am very fond of simplicity in medicine.

ZIMMERMANN.

That is, because your majesty is accustomed to execute the grandest enterprises by the simplest means.

FREDERIC.

The more complex the machinery employed in

* *Cagliostro le Fripon, l'Aveugle, et le Schaman de Syberie de sa Majesté l'Impératrice de Russie.* Berlin chez Nicolai, 1788.

† Frederic always entertained the same opinion. After his death, my friend count Luchesini wrote to me, on the 16th of September 1786, "The empress of Russia, at one time the friend of Frederic, and at another the rival of his glory, was always the subject of the discourse and admiration of this singular prince. I shall ever remember, with pleasure, the conversations which I had with him respecting this great and enterprising sovereign; and when circumstances will permit me to undertake any work relative to the life of Frederic, I will not be afraid of displeasing her by publishing it."

in any work, the greater danger there is that ſome parts of it may be deranged, and deſtroy the whole.

His majeſty concluded his converſation by aſſuring me, that he would continue to take my remedy. At three after dinner, I found him ſtill very cheerful and in good humour. He had, however, an hour before, been again attacked by the colic.

FREDERIC.

The colic is owing to my having eaten too much melon at dinner.

ZIMMERMANN.

Melons are not ſo hurtful alone, as when eaten with other food.

FREDERIC.

Do you know the ſmall green African melon, the pulp of which is white? It ſurpaſſes every other kind in delicacy, flavour, and taſte.

ZIMMERMANN.

We have not that melon at Hanover, though we have all foreign fruits, as ſucculent as poſſible.

FREDERIC.

To-morrow I will ſend you ſome of theſe melons, and you will then ſee how difficult it is to reſiſt temptation.

June

June 30th.—This morning his majeſty was again in very good humour, and I took advantage of that opportunity to ſpeak to him reſpecting his diet. He aſſigned a reaſon for every thing he did; converſed very rationally on a proper regimen; and aſſured me that he would obſerve it with the utmoſt attention; that he would abſtain from what was hurtful and of bad digeſtion; and that he would be contented with only taſting each diſh. He then recurred to melons, and told me that at noon he would ſend me one from his table, which he did. When we had converſed ſome time on diet, his majeſty turned the converſation to other objects.

FREDERIC.

Do you find much change in Potſdam, ſince you ſaw it fifteen years ago?

ZIMMERMANN.

Yes—ſince that period your majeſty has cauſed a great number of new buildings to be erected. The city is ornamented in every quarter. I often imagine that I am at Rome, Vicenza, or Venice, and not in Germany. Beſides palaces, the ſmall houſes, which your majeſty has cauſed to be built, pleaſe me very much. If individuals poſſeſſed good taſte, and were fond of it, they might eaſily imitate that

manner

manner of building. I greatly wiſh that our architects of Lower Saxony would come hither to learn their trade. Architecture there is ſtill in its infancy. It appears to me that theſe pretty little houſes would not coſt more than our *wooden boxes* at Hanover: beſides, their decorations are of ſuch a nature as to reſiſt the inclemencies of the weather.

FREDERIC.

Their decorations are of cut ſtone, if you pleaſe.

ZIMMERMANN.

I obſerve that I have committed a blunder, and I beg your majeſty's pardon.

FREDERIC.

I am fond of building, and I build a great deal.

ZIMMERMANN.

By that your majeſty not only puts your reſidence on a footing with the fineſt cities of Europe; but you alſo relieve all the poor people in your kingdom, and give houſes to thoſe who have none.

FREDERIC.

I never experience more pleaſure than when I build a houſe for a poor man.

At two in the afternoon I received a viſit, at

at Potſdam, from one of thoſe who had the honour of being admitted to his majeſty's table, and who told me very bad news. Frederic, at dinner, had paid little attention to thoſe rules reſpecting his diet, of which he had boaſted ſo much in the morning. He had firſt eaten a large quantity of ſoup, compoſed of ſtrong and extremely hot ingredients; and he had added to it, as uſual, a large ſpoonful of ginger, nutmeg, and other ſpices. After his ſoup, he had eaten heartily of *bouilli à la Ruſſe*, that is to ſay, dreſſed with a pint of ſpirits: and after this, an Italian diſh, compoſed of the flour of Turkey-corn and Parmeſan cheeſe. To this is added the juice of garlic: it is then fried in butter, until a cruſt is formed upon it as thick as one's finger; and it is then ſeaſoned with the ſtrongeſt ſpices. This diſh, invented firſt by lord Marſhal, and afterwards improved by the king himſelf, is called Polenta. In ſhort, while boaſting of the wonderful appetite which the dandelion had given him, his majeſty ended his repaſt by eating a whole plateful of eel-pie, which was ſo hot, that his companion at table told me and my wife, *that it looked as if it had been baked in hell.*

The effect of the king's wonderful appetite began to appear even at dinner. The good humour and cheerfulneſs of the morning had vaniſhed; his majeſty fell into a ſlumber, and convulſive motions again appeared on his countenance. When he awoke, he had ſome retchings; and the company left table an hour ſooner than uſual. I had no reaſon to doubt, that Frederic had already curſed Zimmermann and his dandelion a hundred times. The ſtorm, however, was much more dreadful than I expected. At three I ſet forward to wait upon his majeſty, as I had been ordered, very much diſcouraged, with ſome degree of peeviſhneſs, and, I muſt freely confeſs, with a great deal of reluctance.

His looks were indeed terrible. In the large hollows of his cheeks, and on his lips, which were uſually very beautiful and agreeable, I perceived marks of the deepeſt and moſt profound ſadneſs. The firſt words which he ſpoke made me tremble. In writing this work, I heſitated a long time whether I ſhould not ſuppreſs them, out of regard for thoſe who ſacrifice every thing to external appearance, and who affect to ſhew greatneſs of ſoul even in their meaneſt actions: but having reflected, that the greateſt men, thoſe even placed upon a throne, and thoſe who are in a ſituation calculated to fix the attention of the public, have, like us poor *miniatures of men*, moments of peeviſhneſs and melancholy, which they expreſs in the ſame manner, I concluded, that I ought not to conceal, that the greateſt character of the eighteenth century, Frederic the Great, at three o'clock after dinner, on the 30th of June, 1786, ſaid to me, *I am now only an old carcaſe, fit to be thrown to the dogs.*

On hearing this expreſſion, I replied, with ſome emotion, " Your majeſty ſurveys only the worſt ſide of the affair : you forget thoſe lucid and favourable intervals which you have often had, and even enjoyed this morning : you forget what you are, and what you have done, through the whole courſe of your life, for your kingdom, and for thoſe who live under your government : theſe critical and melancholy moments will paſs, and then your majeſty will ſoon recover your former ſtrength and vivacity of mind. Your lower belly, ſire, is at preſent full and diſtended ; to-morrow, when you have had a couple of ſtools, your wonted gaiety will return."

During the whole time I converſed with him, his majeſty looked eagerly at me, as uſual, and with eyes ſuch as were, perhaps, never formed for any royal head : but whilſt I was concluding my diſcourſe he moved aſide his face. As I continued to ſpeak to him in a tender but firm tone of voice, he turned his eyes inſenſibly towards me, and at length fixed them upon me with an expreſſion of contentment, and even of friendſhip. This quarter of an hour, the commencement of which was very terrible, ended by being one of the happieſt of my whole life.

July 1.—At eight in the morning, the king was ſtill melancholy, and dejected, but much leſs than the evening before; and the ſound of his voice was very mild and agreeable.* He ſpoke to me in ſo friendly and polite a manner, that the tears were ready to ſtart from my eyes: he often called me my dear ſir, my good ſir, my dear Mr. Zimmermann, and even my dear friend. Our converſation ended by the following dialogue, which contains ſome ſtrokes that appear to me to be very characteriſtic.

FREDERIC.

Some days happineſs has paſſed away very quickly.

ZIMMERMANN.

Your majeſty really cannot bear and digeſt your food.

* An ingenious Engliſh traveller has ſaid, and with much truth, "His tone of voice is the cleareſt, and moſt agreeable in converſation I ever heard."

FREDERIC.

To-day, however, I have experienced a very affecting pleaſure. Some letters I have received bring me the agreeable intelligence, that the crop will not be ſo bad in my dominions, as I had reaſon to apprehend.

Perceiving what his majeſty's thoughts were employed on, I ſpoke no more of diet, but of the weather. The king then took off his hat according to cuſtom, for fear, without doubt, that I might recur to the ſubject of diet, and ſaid to me, in a very friendly manner, " Adieu, my dear ſir: be ſo kind as return at three."

At three o'clock.—His majeſty had been relieved by ſeveral abundant ſtools, and I found him in very good humour. He converſed with me a long time upon different ſubjects; and very luckily did not ſay a ſingle word reſpecting medicine.

FREDERIC.

From what part of Swiſſerland do you come?

ZIMMERMANN.

From the ſmall city of Brug, in the canton of Berne.

FREDERIC.

I do not know that place.

ZIMMERMANN.

It is a place where the victories and fate of

your majeſty have made me paſs many an anxious night.

FREDERIC.

Are there ſtill in Swiſſerland any of the deſcendants of the firſt founders of the republic?

To this queſtion I really could not reply; but as I knew that his majeſty did not love an indeciſive anſwer, I boldly ſaid, No.

FREDERIC.

William Tell was a great benefactor to his country.

ZIMMERMANN.

Tell, and his companions, did the greateſt ſervice that can be rendered to a country. To theſe heroes we are indebted for our liberty.

FREDERIC.

I am very fond of republican conſtitutions; the preſent age, however, is dangerous for all republics: Swiſſerland alone ſeems likely ſtill to ſubſiſt long. I love the Swiſs, and above all the government of Berne. There is dignity in every thing which that government does. I love the people of Berne.

ZIMMERMANN.

What your majeſty has juſt now ſaid, renders me proud and happy—I ſhall never forget it. All

All republics, however, are not worthy of your majesty's esteem—for example, Holland—

FREDERIC.

The king of France rules, and commands, as much in Amsterdam as in Champagne.

ZIMMERMANN.

And the Dutch at present have been seized with a fever and phrenzy, which will ever disgrace the words patriot and patriotism.

FREDERIC.

That is true; but, however, I am displeased also....... Here the king told me several very important things, with a confidence that surprised me; and at the same time was so good as to add, *let that be spoken under the rose*. Luckily he forgot his condition whilst he was conversing on this and other subjects: but I recurred to it, by begging him to resume the dandelion next morning. His majesty replied, by telling me, that he had no confidence in that medicine. He, however, promised to take it next morning.

July 2.—The king had taken his remedy, and he informed me, that he found himself well: he was indeed in good humour; but I had previously learned the cause of it in the antichamber. Very early in the morning he had ordered for his dinner a macaroni pie.

This morning was extremely cheerful for his majesty, and consequently for me. He spoke with as much vivacity as ever he did when in perfect health. I am sorry that both honour and duty prevent me from relating the greater part of the things which he said to me. He took a general survey of all the crowned heads in Europe, and after asked me, if I knew this or the other German prince. He mentioned a great number, of whom I knew only a part; but I said all the good of them that I could. Frederic brought them all to trial, and gave them such *severe cuts*, that, notwithstanding my reserve, it was impossible for me not to laugh sometimes. I plainly perceived that my smiles did not escape his majesty, whose full eye never lost sight of me for a moment, and that they did not displease him. I shall mention only one of those princes, to give some idea of this interesting conversation, and to shew what I ventured to say to Frederic respecting our philosophy. His majesty having said something in favour of that prince, I replied, that he was very amiable.

FREDERIC.

He does not pleaſe me altogether; he is too intriguing.

ZIMMERMANN.

They ſay alſo, that he is rather too ſuperſtitious.

FREDERIC.

Yes, he is very ſuperſtitious. He has entered into all the follies of alchymy and theurgy; and theſe, as you know, have had their origin in free-maſonry. I laugh at all theſe follies.

ZIMMERMANN.

The ſmile of a ſovereign is often the beſt of laws; at leaſt, it is always the mildeſt.

FREDERIC.

The progreſs of reaſon has almoſt every where deſtroyed ſuperſtition.

ZIMMERMANN.

Yes—at Vienna, ſire; but it is very ſtrange to ſee, in countries more enlightened than Auſtria, ſuperſtition ſupport itſelf, and ſtill ſpread, as in the ages of the moſt profound ignorance.

FREDERIC.

Superſtition, however, ſeldom makes its way to monarchs. But ſeveral of our learned men are ſuperſtitious. What do you think of *unknown ſuperiors*, Mr. Zimmermann?

ZIMMER-

ZIMMERMANN.

I consider these *unknown superiors* as cast-off preceptors, or bankrupt authors.

FREDERIC.

Have you any of these enthusiasts at Hanover?

ZIMMERMANN.

One of them came from Berlin to Hanover last year. He fell in love with all the women, and railed against enthusiasts of every kind, though he himself was one of the greatest. He rolled about his eyes in a frightful manner; his visage appeared sometimes red, sometimes pale; and he made use of such grimaces and gesticulation in my house, that one would have thought there were jesuits concealed under all my tables and chests of drawers. He beseeched me, in the name of God, to write to the empress of Russia, to warn her to be on her guard against the jesuitical serpents whom she cherished in her bosom.

His majesty afterwards spoke of the catholic princes, and I took that opportunity to introduce the Pope. With regard to the latter, Frederic said very laconically, *It is all over with him.*

At three after dinner, the macaroni pie began

gan to produce its effect, and gave rise to the following converſation.

FREDERIC.

It appears to me, that the dandelion which I take is only a *fiddle faddle* kind of a medicine.

ZIMMERMANN.

Your majeſty ſurely does not imagine that I would dare to order you *medicinal baubles*: but we cannot attack a diſorder, ſuch as that of your majeſty, in a direct manner.

FREDERIC.

I am ſenſible of that: for if you did ſo, you would deſtroy the patient.

In ſhort the king was very polite and friendly; and he promiſed to reſume the dandelion next morning.

July 3. This morning the king had taken his medicine, and appeared to be tolerably well, and in good humour. The evening before, he ſaid to Count Lucheſini, and thoſe who had been in company with him, "Zimmermann has nothing of the quack about him; he is quite different from every phyſician I know. One may converſe with him on all ſubjects; I am obliged to him, and am perfectly ſatisfied with his behaviour."

How-

However little I merited, or may ever merit ſuch praiſe, I think it my duty not to paſs it over in ſilence, becauſe I am too old to fear mankind; becauſe it forms a part of this narrative; and becauſe it inſpired me with courage and confidence in my viſits to the king. On theſe occaſions I took advantage of thoſe moments, when his majeſty ſpoke only of medicine, to tell him a great many uſeful truths.

After dinner Frederic ſeemed very well, and in the beſt humour poſſible. A little before I arrived, he had inhaled the vapour ariſing from an infuſion of elder flowers in vinegar, which I ordered him with a view to render his reſpiration eaſier. This remedy had given him ſo much relief, that he boaſted of its good effects to his company, as well as to myſelf; adding, that he had found much benefit from the clyſter I had preſcribed in the morning.

We then talked of diet, and I ſaid every thing on this ſubject, that I thought uſeful, or neceſſary. His majeſty approved of the whole, and our converſation ended as follows.

FREDERIC.

I allow that my ſtomach is not capable of bearing melons.

ZIMMER-

ZIMMERMANN.

I and my ſpouſe finiſhed to-day the ſmall African melon, which your majeſty ſent me four days ago. You ſee, ſire, that I obſerve the ſame regimen which I recommend to my patients.

FREDERIC.

You have then ſeen how much my Chriſtian ſoul muſt be tormented by reſiſting ſuch a temptation.

ZIMMERMANN.

It appears that your majeſty cannot bear fruits which do not relax, and that is the caſe with melons. Your majeſty ought to eat grapes, becauſe they purge gently; and you always find yourſelf better after eating things which produce that effect.

FREDERIC.

You are right—grapes are the only fruit I can bear.

ZIMMERMANN.

Grapes are, in many reſpects, a wholeſome fruit; but in the north they can be preſcribed only for few people, becauſe there are no vines.

FREDERIC.

Have you never ſeen the vineyards of my country?

ZIMMER-

ZIMMERMANN.

I was agreeably furprifed on feeing the vines which are on the road between Brandenburg and Potfdam. I had travelled from Magdeburg a great way acrofs fands, and was charmed to find all of a fudden, near the city of Werder, a very rich and well-cultivated country, which made me forget the fands.

FREDERIC.

Mankind are vain enough to imagine that every thing in the world was created for them; and yet I cannot conceive why God created fands.

I could not help fmiling at this obfervation of his majefty: it appeared to me fo natural, and at the fame time fo pleafant, that an elector of Brandenburg fhould confefs, with fo much *naiveté*, that he could not conceive why God had created fands. My fmile embarraffed him for a moment.

FREDERIC.

I am very well fatisfied with the induftry of my fubjects in that canton. There are vineyards alfo in Silefia: wines are made there every year, to the value of three hundred thoufand crowns. Part of this wine is employed, it is true, in making vinegar; and the other, adulterated by different fubftances, is tranfported to Stettin,

Stettin, from whence it is imported under the name of Pontac.

ZIMMERMANN.

Pontac made at Bremen, Hamburg, and Lubec, with berries from the heaths of Lunenburg, is ſold alſo at Hanover.

FREDERIC.

Have you ſeen here the vineyard of Dr. Freſe ?*

ZIMMERMANN.

I was much pleaſed both with the vineyard and its owner.

FREDERIC.

That vineyard brings three hundred crowns annually to the proprietor.

ZIMMER-

* Counſellor Freſe was phyſician to the court and the garriſon of Potſdam. He is a man of great ability and judgment. The king had often ſent for him, in order to conſult him reſpecting his health; and Mr. Freſe always gave him proper and uſeful advice, with the uſual ſucceſs: but though I much wiſhed for it, the king did not ſee Mr. Freſe during my whole ſtay at Potſdam. His majeſty hated conſultations, becauſe he believed, and certainly not without reaſon, that phyſicians never ſought them but for the purpoſe of charging each other with the conſequences. He preferred hearing each phyſician ſeparately, *ad protocollum*. Mr. Freſe was of great ſervice to me, becauſe the king had ſent him, about the concluſion of the war of ſeven years, to Baktſchiſarai, to cure the then reigning chan of the Tartars, of a pain in his head, which he effectually did.

Some

ZIMMERMANN.

I tafted fome of the wine which it produces; it is of a very beautiful red colour; but I found it horribly harfh and four.

FREDERIC.

For that reafon I will make you tafte my grapes.

His majefty then called one of his domeftics; and having ordered him to bring a plateful of grapes, he picked out the fineft, and defired me to eat them.

ZIMMERMANN.

Thefe are equal to the beft grapes of Neufchatel.

Some years before, the king had begun a negociation in the Crimea, to engage the chan to fall upon the Ruffians with all his hordes. The chan replied, that he would do it very willingly, but that it would be firft neceffary to fend him a phyfician to cure his diforder; and with this view his majefty fent Mr. Frefe. The moment, however, when he had effected the cure, the emprefs Elizabeth died, and Ruffia became an ally of Pruffia. The death of the emprefs, and this revolution, greatly chagrined the chan; and he ftill wifhed, fpite of every oppofition, to enter Ruffia with an army of an hundred thoufand Tartars; fo that Frederic was obliged to difpatch courier after courier, to prevent his friend the chan from purfuing this meafure, and to convince him that it would be then a piece of great folly.

FRE-

FREDERIC.

With your permiſſion, they grow in my green-houſe.

After converſing about half an hour more on different ſubjects, the king ſaid, "Adieu, my "dear and worthy ſir;" adding, with a ſmile, "I recommend myſelf to your protection and "good providence."

July 4th. This morning, at eight, Frederic was in charming humour.

FREDERIC.

I am very well pleaſed with your dandelion; it gives me an excellent appetite, and keeps my belly open. I will continue it with great pleaſure.

ZIMMERMANN.

Yeſterday morning, and to-day, I took the liberty of ordering your majeſty, without your knowledge, three ſpoonfuls, inſtead of two, of the juice of dandelion.

FREDERIC.

I am ſatisfied. When I take medicines I know very well that I take diſagreeable things; and I ſwallow them quickly, without attending to the taſte. I have again uſed your vapour, with which I am alſo pleaſed, and I will continue it.

Here the king raiſed his arm; and, with a very ſignificant geſture, ſaid, *But ſeventy-five!*

ZIMMERMANN.

A life like that of your majeſty is not to be reckoned by the number of years.

FREDERIC.

I will mount on horſeback to-day at eleven; Mr. Zimmermann, I recommend myſelf - - -

At three in the afternoon I found the king in the moſt painful ſituation: every thing was changed and become worſe. When in good humour, he had taken his dandelion and drank coffee: after this, he had applied, from half after three in the morning till ſeven, to public buſineſs. Great part of the morning he had ſpent in eating; for as ſoon as I left him, a plate of ſweet-meats, compoſed of ſugar, whites of eggs, and cream, had been brought him, one of which I ate, and found the cream very ſour. His majeſty ate the whole plateful for his breakfaſt; and afterwards ſtrawberries, cherries, and cold meat. At eleven his ſervants found great difficulty in getting him on horſeback. He remained there three hours, in the great garden of *Sans Souci*, galloped almoſt the whole time, and returned very much weakened and exhauſted. When he ſat down to table he had

no

no appetite; and immediately after dinner he was ſeized with a vomiting.

At three I found him ſo ill, and ſo much oppreſſed, that he could not ſpeak; and he diſmiſſed me by ſaying, "Forgive me, ſir; I really cannot ſpeak."—I therefore talked to Mr. Schœning reſpecting what I thought likely to be of uſe to his majeſty, and to relieve his immediate complaints.

July 5th The king was much better than he had been the day before, after dinner; he however complained of a conſtriction and heavineſs at his ſtomach. I adviſed him to take a doſe of his digeſtive powder, which was his favourite remedy.

FREDERIC.

I have a pain in my eyes.

ZIMMERMANN.

There is too much light in your apartment; if agreeable to your majeſty, I will draw one of the curtains.

FREDERIC.

No, no—I have always been fond of light.

ZIMMERMANN.

Your majeſty likewiſe has always diffuſed it every where around you.

FREDERIC.

For all that, I never was any thing but a poor mortal.

I then began to ſpeak of his majeſty's ſituation, which appeared to me to be very critical. He however always reſumed courage.

FREDERIC.

Hitherto we have only ſkirmiſhed with the enemy; we have not overcome him.

ZIMMERMANN.

We muſt always renew the attack, and never ſuffer him to be at reſt.

FREDERIC.

Your manner of carrying on war pleaſes me much.

After examining his pulſe, I ſaid—

ZIMMERMANN.

Your pulſe is good, and far from being weak; whilſt it continues in that ſtate, every ſymptom of great weakneſs will be only temporary. Yeſterday, in the forenoon, the afternoon, and at night, your majeſty was extremely weak; at preſent no traces of weakneſs are to be ſeen: and this proves that there is ſtill vigour in the heart.

FREDERIC (*ſmiling*).

Do you know the reaſon of that? It is be-

cauſe

caufe my father never had the venereal difeafe. Have you never obferved thofe feeble fpectres, who are fo common in France, and who fuffer fo dreadfully for the fins of their fathers?

ZIMMERMANN.

I have feen fome of them at Paris, and in other places. They are true pictures of death; but though the Englifh are as great libertines, and perhaps more fo than the French (for the latter are libertines by temperament, whereas the Englifh are fo by principle, and becaufe it is fafhionable), yet thefe iflanders are always more vigorous than the French.

FREDERIC.

That is owing to their eating more nourifhing food than the French; though, on the other hand, I cannot conceive how a piece of half roafted meat, all bloody, can give ftrength.

This day his majefty difmiffed me in fuch a manner as induced me to believe, that I fhould obtain permiffion to return to Hanover: for he faid, when I left him, "I hope, my dear fir, that "you will be fo kind as to return in the after-"noon, that I may thank you for the attention "which you have paid to me."

When I returned, after dinner, it appeared that the king had changed his opinion: for no mention was made of my departure. He complained ſtill of a conſtriction and weight in the lower belly; telling me, at the ſame time, that he was much troubled with wind: he was likewiſe in very bad humour, as may be ſeen by our converſation.

FREDERIC.

Your dandelion has performed nothing; I find myſelf no better ſince I began to take it.

ZIMMERMANN.

Your majeſty ought to remember, that I propoſed this remedy merely to relieve you, and not with any hope of its performing a complete cure. You have not uſed it long enough to be relieved; and, by not taking it regularly, you have deſtroyed all its good effects.

FREDERIC.

It is true, you told me at firſt that I could not hope for any relief from dandelion, unleſs I continued to take it for a whole month.

Our converſation was very ſhort; and his majeſty diſmiſſed me with theſe fatal and expreſſive words—*Adieu, Mr. Phyſician* *.

At ſix o'clock, when the company who form-

* Always when the king was in bad humour he called me *Mr. Phyſician*; at other times he never made uſe of this expreſſion.

ed his evening party arrived, he immediately dismissed them, by saying, " Gentlemen, I shall be in too bad humour this evening."

July 6th. The king was a little easier, and in much better humour.

FREDERIC.

I do not find that I am cured by your dandelion.

ZIMMERMANN.

My intention in giving your majesty advice was, to afford you relief; and by the use of this medicine to prevent, as much as possible, the dropsy; but it will not prevent your majesty from being oppressed by indigestion, when you eat improper food.

FREDERIC.

But I have not the dropsy.

ZIMMERMANN.

It may soon come on, and we ought to do every thing we can to guard against it.

FREDERIC.

I fear no danger: but I do not like to suffer pain; I wish for a remedy that would cure me instantaneously.

ZIMMERMANN.

I wish with all my heart that I could ad-minifter fuch a remedy to your majefty; but I know not where to find it.

FREDERIC.

Let every thing then happen as it may—I am not afraid of death, but of pain.

Adieu, Mr. Phyfician.

At three the king was again attacked by a colic, the confequence of indigeftion; and he was in very bad humour. At dinner he had eaten plentifully of frefh eels, and yet he afcribed his colic to dandelion. He railed therefore againft *Mr. Phyfician* and the dandelion. This occafioned a converfation which I luckily diverted, by fixing the king's imagination for a few moments upon other objects.

FREDERIC *(in a very morofe tone).*

Did your Hanoverian foldiers fwallow any of this dandelion at Gibraltar?

ZIMMERMANN.

No, fire; they fubftituted in its ftead Malaga and Port wine.

FREDERIC.

The Hanoverians diftinguifhed themfelves very much by their conduct at Gibraltar. How did they behave in the Eaft Indies?

ZIMMERMANN.

Immediately on their arrival, they performed very

very long marches, before they were accuſtomed to the great heat; ſeveral of them died therefore by being ſun-ſtruck. After theſe dreadful marches they fought very badly againſt the French. At preſent they are ſo ſeaſoned to the climate, that they have no deſire to return. Your majeſty ſees that the Hanoverian troops are ſtill the ſame, and that they always behave with bravery in India as well as at Gibraltar.

Adieu, Mr. Phyſician.

July 7th. For ſeveral days ſucceſſively the king had taken ſome of his dear digeſtive powder; and afterwards rhubarb, and glauber ſalts, which I thought much more proper. Yeſterday evening ſeveral ſtrong ſtools had diſpelled for a moment all his bad humour. "A new remedy," ſays his majeſty, "has juſt arrived, "which I mean to try at noon; this remedy," added he, "is freſh herrings." I congratulated his majeſty on his new remedy, and begged him not to forget rhubarb and glauber ſalts, after which I was diſmiſſed at the uſual hour. After dinner, the king was not ſo well as he had been in the morning; but he behaved with much politeneſs.

FREDERIC.

I have reflected a good deal upon what you ſaid yeſterday, reſpecting the dropſy, which from

from your hints I have reaſon to apprehend. I am now convinced that you are right; for I preſſed my legs with my finger, and the part remained hollow. This is an evident ſymptom of the dropſy.

ZIMMERMANN.

Many people perform the ſame experiment, and with the like ſymptoms, for ten years, and yet are not dropſical.

FREDERIC.

O! do not ſpeak to me of hopes!

ZIMMERMANN.

I ſhall ſay nothing elſe than that your majeſty coughs leſs, and labours under leſs oppreſſion.

FREDERIC.

That is true; but my lower belly is in a bad ſtate.

ZIMMERMANN.

All thoſe uneaſy ſenſations in the lower belly, of which your majeſty ſo often complains, do not always ariſe directly from your diſorder; but depend upon cauſes altogether accidental, and well known to your majeſty.

FREDERIC.

At preſent I ſuffer much from tenſion and ſpaſms.

ZIMMER-

ZIMMERMANN.

Your majeſty ſhould take a little mint water.

FREDERIC.

Will mint water give me inſtant relief?

ZIMMERMANN.

It will relieve you as much, and as ſoon, as any thing.

FREDERIC.

Adieu, Mr. Phyſician.

July 8th. The king had ſlept five hours without interruption, and found himſelf tolerably well this morning. He complained however of diſtenſion.

FREDERIC.

I am certain that I ſhall be attacked alſo with the tympany and dropſy.

ZIMMERMANN.

Your majeſty has nothing to fear from the windy dropſy; and the ordinary dropſy may be cured by proper remedies.

FREDERIC.

I deſire no remedies, nor will I take any, unleſs they relieve me, and perform an immediate cure. The mint water which you preſcribed yeſterday has not expelled my flatulencies.

ZIMMERMANN.

Alas! we have few ſpecific remedies; and even

even theſe do not always perform a cure, or operate inſtantaneouſly. We phyſicians are poor mortals.

FREDERIC.

You nevertheleſs abound in preſcriptions.

ZIMMERMANN.

I muſt make one obſervation, which I am confident is very juſt :—Your majeſty's moſt dangerous enemies are your cooks.

FREDERIC.

You cannot form any idea of my temperance. I only taſte my food, and eat merely for the ſake of acquiring ſtrength.

ZIMMERMANN.

I firmly believe in the truth of another obſervation, which is, that people are never ſtrengthened but by what they digeſt.

FREDERIC.

That is very true.

ZIMMERMANN.

You majeſty's cook is a great man in his way; but I conſider him as a very dangerous man*.

FREDERIC.

* This great man, Mr. Noel, is known by an Epiſtle, printed ſome years ago, which the king addreſſed to him, under the title of the Emperor of China, to thank him for

a new

FREDERIC.

No people know better how to form good cooks than your Hanoverian miniſters. My cook is from their ſchool.

ZIMMERMANN.

Our miniſters entertain their gueſts in a moſt ſplendid and ſumptuous manner; but they themſelves live very temperately.

FREDERIC.

I ſaw here Mr. de Lichtenſtein, one of your miniſters, with wnom I was much pleaſed.

ZIMMERMANN.

Mr. de Lichtenſtein is firſt marſhal of the court. He poſſeſſes much knowledge of the world, and is a very amiable character. I often viſit him, becauſe I am his phyſician, and becauſe the marſhals of the court are fond of living in cloſe intimacy with their phyſicians.

FREDERIC.

Laſt year I ſaw alſo Mr. de Buelwiz, the Hanoverian envoy.

a new diſh (*Bombe à la Sardanapale*) which he had invented. Before I knew this Mr. Noel, I had an opportunity of ſeeing him, one day, at a public concert at Potſdam. The air of importance which was diſplayed in his countenance ſtruck me much, though I could ſee nothing grand in it. After being informed by an officer who he was, I told him that I perceived by his looks that an emperor of China had written to him.

ZIMMER-

ZIMMERMANN.

He was ſent to your majeſty on account of the league of the German princes; and that affair lay very heavy on his heart.

FREDERIC.

In this reſpect, Mr. de Buelwiz thought like a good German patriot.

ZIMMERMANN.

By that pacific league, your majeſty crowned all your other noble exploits.

FREDERIC.

Germany is a kind of republic: it was in danger of loſing the republican form; and it was with the ſincereſt pleaſure that I ſaw it re-eſtabliſhed.

Our converſation laſted an hour and a quarter, during which the king ſpoke a great deal, and in a very friendly manner; but he was from time to time incommoded by the tenſion of his lower belly.

After a moderate dinner, Frederic was obliged to vomit, and at four I found him very much dejected, and dozing. He told me that his flatulencies would carry him to the grave. I begged him to take a table-ſpoonful of the tincture of rhubarb, with a few drops of Hoffmann's anodyne, and to repeat this eaſy remedy at at certain periods. His cough had again returned this morning; and count Luchesini told me that in the evening it had been extremely violent.

July 9th. This day the king was easy, and in good humour. "I find myself very well," said he, "owing to the remedy I took yester-"day evening. It purged me several times, "and even in the night." The spasms of the preceding day had disappeared; his majesty did not cough at all; and he experienced very little tension in his belly.

FREDERIC.

After reflecting upon what has happened to me lately, I really believe that I brought on indigestion by eating fresh herrings.

His majesty always ascribed his indigestion to every other cause than the real; for, besides herrings, he had eaten a great many hurtful things.

ZIMMERMANN.

Herrings cannot have done much hurt to your majesty, unless you have eaten more than you could digest: in my opinion, therefore, your majesty ought to blame some other nourishment for the uneasiness and illness which you have experienced some days past.

This morning his majesty had resumed his

 tincture

tincture of rhubarb, with ſome drops of the anodyne. A few grains, about fifteen of the former root, were ſufficient to purge him. Rhubarb ſeemed in general to agree very well with him; and on this account he was ſo fond of it, that he preſcribed it once to Gellert, and very often to his ſoldiers.—At three in the afternoon I found the king much worſe than he had been in the morning, becauſe he had eaten too much at dinner. The tincture of rhubarb had however brought back his wonted good humour; for he appeared very cheerful, and his thoughts ſucceeded each other with wonderful rapidity. One idea immediately ſucceeded another; and our converſation continued, without interruption, for two hours. Of all thoſe I had with Frederic, none was more intereſting; but unluckily I am obliged to ſuppreſs the greater part of it. The beginning of it was as follows:

FREDERIC.

(Very penſive, and with his head inclined to one ſide). The examination of an important and complex affair is exceſſively difficult.

ZIMMERMANN.

Since the creation of the world, no one poſ-

ſeſſed

ſeſſed that art in greater perfection than your majeſty.

FREDERIC.

A kingdom greater than France cannot well be governed.

ZIMMERMANN.

Either the people of the provinces do not obey government, or the governors do what pleaſes them rather than what they are commanded to do.

FREDERIC.

Ruſſia is too vaſt and extenſive an empire.

ZIMMERMANN.

Not for a woman of ſo much courage and ſpirit as Catherine; but at ſome future period this empire may ſink under its own weight.

FREDERIC.

Do not imagine that.

ZIMMERMANN.

The Ruſſian empire may one day be divided, as that of Alexander was after his death. The governors of provinces may erect themſelves into kings of thoſe provinces, and make war on the neighbouring governors who have followed their example.

FREDERIC.

In that you are right; I entertain the ſame opinion.—The king ſpoke afterwards of other countries and empires; but I am obliged to ſtop here. I am well enough acquainted with mankind to know, that I may have perhaps ſaid many things to this great prince, which people of ordinary talents, and leſs knowledge of the world, neither could have borne nor digeſted. I was at firſt, as I naturally am, very reſerved; and when his majeſty turned the converſation to political matters, I made no anſwer, and was contented with liſtening. This however was of no avail; for his majeſty always ſtopped when he had delivered his opinion: and when he came to the end of his period, he looked at me with much vivacity, which was as much as to ſay that he wiſhed me to ſpeak. I was then abſolutely under the neceſſity of replying; and the freer, more deciſive, and firm that my anſwers were, the more they ſeemed to pleaſe him.

This converſation appeared at firſt as if likely to be philoſophical; but it became political, and continued an hour. At length, by thoſe ſudden tranſitions which are very common, it became medicinal for another hour. This part I ſhall relate entire; for, though it was upon

medicinal

medicinal objects, I considered it as no less remarkable.

FREDERIC.

What diseases are at present most prevalent in Hanover?

ZIMMERMANN.

Of acute diseases those fevers, above all, which in France are called bilious fevers, but which are known to the German physicians by other names. We have also very frequently putrid and malignant fevers, which are very dangerous.

FREDERIC.

These diseases are more uncommon in my country.

ZIMMERMANN.

Your majesty's armies, and those cities which had numerous garrisons, suffered much by them. In the war of 1778 and 1779 some of these fevers prevailed among your majesty's troops, as well as dysenteries, which were also very common.

FREDERIC.

That is true.—Will you believe me when I tell you that I cured the dysentery very well during the last war? Being in a small town with a body of my troops, the greater part of them were attacked by this disorder, and a number of them died. Though I am not fond of meddling with phyfic, I could not help turning phyfician, when I found that thofe who profeffed it were entirely ignorant of their art. I therefore faid to them, "Diffolve a few grains of emetic tartar in a fufficient quantity of water, and make your patients fwallow a table-fpoonful of it, until they vomit copioufly, and are ftrongly purged." The furgeons did fo, and the remedy fucceeded.

ZIMMERMANN.

Your prefcription was perfectly right.

FREDERIC.

But prefcriptions will not do the whole; much depends upon proper regulations. In all the wars I carried on, my orders refpecting the fick and wounded foldiers were very ill obferved. Nothing, in the whole courfe of my life, ever pained me fo much, as when I faw that the difeafes and wounds of my brave foldiers, who expofed their lives fo nobly for their country, were neglected. They were too often treated with inhumanity; and on that account a great number of them died for want of care. I was at all times grieved when I faw that I had been the innocent caufe of the death of a foldier: but fince the laft war I have given fo ſtrict orders, that all theſe army ſcoundrels and raſcals will find it very difficult to deceive their ſovereign, and to deprive the poor ſoldiers, in ſo barbarous a manner, of the neceſſary aſſiſtance.

ZIMMERMANN.

That is much to be wiſhed; but I am afraid that your majeſty is as yet acquainted but with a ſmall part of the mal-practices prevalent in your hoſpitals during the courſe of the laſt war.

FREDERIC.

(Opening his large piercing eyes, and fixing them upon me).

I know it, as well as all Germany, from various papers which have been publiſhed. I know it from the author of thoſe papers, who was born in your majeſty's dominions; who ſerved faithfully and honourably under prince Henry in Saxony; and who had no other reward for his fidelity than to be perſecuted, hated, and oppreſſed, by ſome of his brethren at Berlin.

FREDERIC.

What is his name?

ZIMMERMANN.

His name is Frize; he is a phyſician at Halberſtadt.

FREDERIC.

Write down his name, if you pleafe.

ZIMMERMANN.

I will write it down in the anti-chamber, as I go out.

FREDERIC.

I do not know Doctor Frize; I never even heard of his name.

ZIMMERMANN.

I am forry for it, on your majefty's account. I know no perfon, fire, more capable of informing your majefty, and in the minuteft manner, refpecting all the tricks and abufes committed in this department. He is a perfon who has feen every thing with his own eyes; he is not afraid to fpeak his fentiments, is an excellent phyfician, and a man of genius.

FREDERIC.

I fet no value on a man of genius, if he is not alfo an honeft man. Tell me, fincerely, is Doctor Frize of Halberftadt a man ftrictly honeft?

ZIMMERMANN.

He is, without doubt. It was his honefty alone which ruined him at Berlin; and it is merely on account of his probity that I take the

the liberty of recommending him to your majesty. But as I am not personally acquainted with him, I do not know whether, with that vivacity for which he is distinguished, he could execute with success what your majesty may require of him; whether he has not something stiff and disagreeable in his manner; whether he is not, perhaps, too hot and violent; and whether he understands how to address people on the most favourable side.

FREDERIC.

That is all the same to me; write down his name.—After this, the king began to turn the conversation to himself; and said, "You must see in what a pitiful manner I walk; come with me."—His hussar being then called, he raised Frederic from his easy chair, and supported him by holding his arm. I followed his majesty, and when he spoke to me I placed myself at his side. In this manner the king traversed three apartments, with much pain and distress. My heart almost bled during this scene. His majesty advanced with the greatest difficulty; he was quite out of breath, though he walked very slowly; and when he spoke, which he did often, I could not understand him. He at length said that he wished to return ; and when we reached the apartment which he uſually occupied, I ſtood up before him. When he recovered, and was in a condition to ſpeak, which was not till ſome time after, our converſation continued thus.

FREDERIC.

Have you at preſent many patients ?

ZIMMERMANN.

At this ſeaſon many Hanoverians and foreigners conſult me reſpecting their ſummer cures.

FREDERIC.

I dare not then detain you any longer here, and deprive your patients of your aſſiſtance. Return, I pray, at eight to-morrow morning, in order that I may thank you for the kind attention which you have paid to me ſo long. I will then give you a letter for his royal highneſs the duke of York.

Before he permitted me to depart, Frederic ſaid, " I believe I ſhall be afflicted alſo with a " hernia, becauſe I have pains of a peculiar kind," which he deſcribed. Thoſe pains, I told him, indicated a quite different thing, and that they generally preceded the hemorrhoids; adding that, however ſingular it might then appear, I was confident the hemorrhoids would ſoon flow.

" That

" That would be very ſerviceable," ſaid the king, taking off his hat with much politeneſs, which was the uſual ſignal for me to depart.

July 10. I received before the door of the king's apartment, from his majeſty's ſecond huſſar, and in his majeſty's name, a thouſand crowns more in bank notes. As ſoon as I entered, Frederic reſumed the converſation which we had been upon before, which at firſt aſtoniſhed me greatly, and in the end affected me much more.

FREDERIC.

You ſignalize yourſelf even to the laſt moment of your reſidence here.

ZIMMERMANN.

An idea of my own weakneſs, and a thorough conviction that I want many things which a phyſician ought to poſſeſs, have always haunted me ſince the firſt moment I attended your majeſty.

FREDERIC.

You are a prophet. When uneaſy yeſterday evening reſpecting certain pains with which I was not acquainted, you told me that they announced the hemorrhoids. Laſt night theſe hemorrhoids made their appearance. I ſlept well;

well; the pains are gone; and I am very much pleaſed with you.

ZIMMERMANN.

One of your majeſty's attendants has juſt now put into my hands a convincing proof that you are ſatisfied with my conduct; a proof which, with what you have ſaid, makes me bluſh, and be ſilent.

FREDERIC.

Do not ſpeak of that, but ſuffer me to return you thanks for your exertions in my favour. You have done every thing that could be done. I am perfectly ſatisfied with you in every reſpect. In returning home will you paſs through Deſſau?

ZIMMERMANN.

Her royal highneſs the princeſs of Deſſau wrote to me at Potſdam, and begged me to ſpend ſome days with her at Woerliz, that ſhe might conſult me reſpecting her health. From thence I will purſue my route, through Antoinnettenruhe and Brunſwick, to Hanover.

FREDERIC.

I aſk pardon of all your patients for having deprived them of your aſſiſtance, and I thank you for your kindneſs in remaining ſo long with me. I wiſh that you may always be happy;

happy; and I am very glad that you have ſeen me, becauſe you may afterwards form a better judgment reſpecting my caſe.

ZIMMERMANN.

I am ſo ſenſibly affected by what your majeſty has ſaid, that I am ſcarcely able to return an anſwer.

FREDERIC.

Be ſo kind, ſir, as to deliver this letter to the duke of York. Tell him how often I have ſpoke to you concerning him; how much I eſteem, and how much I love him. Tell him in my name, and in the ſtrongeſt terms you can, what affection I entertain for him.

ZIMMERMANN.

I will tell the duke, with the utmoſt fidelity, every thing you have ſaid.

The king then took off his hat with much dignity and politeneſs, and in an amicable manner ſaid—"Adieu, my good, my dear Mr. Zimmermann; do not forget the old man whom you have ſeen here."

When his majeſty pronounced theſe words, I was ſo much affected that I could not utter a ſingle ſyllable. I made a profound bow, and quitted the apartment with an emotion ſuch as I never experienced, nor ever can experience, in life.

What

What I have hitherto ſaid, reſpecting the health of Frederic, fills up the vacuum which Mr. Selle, his phyſician in ordinary, left for me in the hiſtory of his majeſty's diſorder, which he has publiſhed; and confirms, beſides, what that able phyſician has ſaid.

At my departure from Potſdam, the king's ſituation was ſo far from being doubtful, that it was really deſperate. He had a dropſy in the breaſt and lower belly; and his thighs and legs were prodigiouſly diſtended with water. According to every appearance, he had an abſceſs in the lungs, where one had appeared the preceding winter. His ſtrength was entirely exhauſted, and he could neither walk nor ſtand upright without being ſupported. His courage however was ſtill great; and when abandoned by hope, in his moments of ſadneſs and dejection, his firmneſs never forſook him entirely. It was impoſſible to do any thing that could really tend to cure him. He himſelf, indeed, expected nothing elſe than to be relieved; to have his appetite preſerved, digeſtion promoted, and his belly kept open. He aſked me only for a ſingle remedy, which was, one that could cure him in an inſtant. I however neither knew nor poſſeſſed ſuch a remedy; and on the 24th of June I renounced all hope of a regular and perfect

perfect cure.—All my conduct towards Frederic, those serious remonstrances which I made to him on the necessity of proper regimen excepted, was at bottom nothing else than *medical policy**.

In the month of August, the king often flattered himself with the idea that his father had lived five years after being attacked by the dropsy; and his majesty's imagination was even then very fertile in consolation.

Between the 4th and 12th of August, the last time that he attended to the business of the cabinet, the swelling in one of his majesty's legs burst. His voice was then exceedingly weak; but he was very attentive to business, and that day eat the half of a sea crab.

On the 17th, thirty-eight days after I had quitted him, he breathed his last. Mr. Selle has perfectly well described the circumstances of his death.

What I have said respecting my conversations with Frederic, leaves nothing else for me

* Dr. Zimmermann here speaks like an honest man. What else is the conduct of many physicians, we will not be so illiberal as to say of all, towards the rich and great, but *medical policy*, to fill their pockets, and extort another fee? There is no period at which mankind will sooner part with their money, than when they are afraid of being compelled to leave it. T.

to do, than to relate ſome intereſting particulars of his character.

The ſtomach, the belly, and the imagination, which, for what reaſon God only knows, depends ſo much on the ſtate of the two former, had more influence over this great man than one might believe. Bad digeſtion rendered him extremely dejected; but when that was over, his wonted vivacity immediately returned. The reader muſt have undoubtedly remarked how he recovered courage on the ſmalleſt change for the better. His invincible incredulity in regard to medicine, made him cry out, a miracle! when a remedy produced the leaſt good effect; and when a phyſician foretold him the moſt trifling circumſtance, he conſidered him as a prophet.

He was often in bad humour during the courſe of his diſorder; yet this bad humour never in my preſence broke out violently except once, on the 24th of June, when I propoſed to have a conſultation with Mr. Selle.

Frederic William I. who alſo died dropſical, was often during his malady in very bad humour; but he expreſſed himſelf in a manner quite different from that of his great ſon, and ſometimes in a manner altogether pious and chriſtianlike.

A certain *naiveté*, not known at preſent, and of which no idea can be formed, prevailed in Germany till the middle of this century, and eſpecially in the beginning of it. The reader will perhaps hardly believe that the ſpouſe of Frederic I. king of Pruſſia wrote to the ſpouſe of George I. at Hanover—

" Leibnitz paſſed the evening with me yeſter-" day, in order to entertain me with his *infiniment* " *petits*. Alas! my dear, who can be better ac-" quainted with them than you or I?"

Frederic William I. poſſeſſed this *naiveté*, but it was altogether German. I do not know whether his illneſs had begun when he drove the citizens of Berlin from the public walk, and ſent them to Spandau, merely becauſe they were fond of walking; when he reduced the penſion of a privy counſellor from a thouſand to four hundred crowns, becauſe, paſſing one evening before his houſe, he had ſeen ſeveral lights in it, and becauſe he learned that this counſellor had company to ſup with him; and, laſtly, when he ſpat one day in a lady's boſom, becauſe he found it too openly diſplayed. But when he was really ill of the dropſy, he made his *valet de chambre* read the evening prayer every night to him when he went to bed. At the end of the prayer there was a benediction.

nediction. One evening the *valet de chambre* read, *May God bless your majesty*; thinking that he ought to read so, from a kind of politeness. "That is not in the book," cried the king, throwing the first thing at him which he could lay his hand upon; "read again." The *valet de chambre*, not knowing in what he could have made a mistake, read again, *May God bless your majesty*.—"It is not so, you scoundrel," cried his majesty once more, throwing his nightcap at him. The poor valet, half dead with fear, read, for the third time, *May God bless your majesty*. His majesty then fell into a dreadful passion; and cried out, "*May God bless you! you* "*scoundrel*—who does not know that, in hea-"ven, I shall be a scoundrel like yourself?"

Frederic the Great, convinced also of his weakness, allowed that mankind are dependent beings; but not with the Germanic *naiveté* of his father, nor in so comico-christian a manner. He felt sensibly, and with an emotion of sadness, what we all are. This hero and conqueror told me, so far back as the year 1771, "Alas! I cannot overcome every obstacle." The same Frederic, the greatest man of the eighteenth century, said to me, in the last summer of his life, "I always was a poor mortal." He who, a little before the gloomy period

riod when he descended among the heroes of antiquity, still ruled his empire with a vigour of mind truly regal, said to me, on the 30th of June 1786, " I am now only an old carcase, fit to be thrown to the dogs."

According to his philosophy, Frederic the Great believed that he owed his existence to chance. He had a just sense, indeed, of his dependence on a superior power, that of age and time: but this great prince had not that consolation which arises to the meanest of mankind. He did not enjoy that comfort which proceeds naturally from our weakness—an idea of our dependence on God, and of the end of our existence beyond this life and the grave. Frederic the Great considered his life as a vapour, created by chance, and which age dissipated. He did not believe in what is the noblest, the best, and the grandest hope of man—the immortality of the soul. His creed was, that the thinking part of man is inseparable from the body, and perishes with it.

He, who was so often melancholy when he reflected how much his existence depended on age and time, was not sensible that this dependence, which renders us so little in one point of view, exalts us in another, by intimately connecting us with the Deity. Frederic the Great, in the latter part of his life, undoubtedly experienced very painful ſenſations. Men generally, either through vanity or affectation, conceal theſe ſenſations; and flatterers, who wiſh to praiſe the great, ſuppoſe that they are never diſturbed by them. This eminent prince did not conceal from me what he felt in this reſpect. Theſe ideas, however, were in his great mind only momentary; and though, for the moſt part, they deſtroy all the activity and faculties of the beſt organized heads, he preſerved, till the laſt moment, his uſual firmneſs and courage. On this account he was always maſter of himſelf. Till almoſt the very moment of his death, he applied, without interruption, to his wonted occupations. It has nevertheleſs been frequently aſſerted, throughout all Germany, that Frederic outlived himſelf; that his powers of mind were exhauſted, and that his vivacity and vigour of thought had abandoned him. It appears to me, on the contrary, that many princes would be very happy to poſſeſs, in the flower of life, that vigour and ſtrength of mind which Frederic enjoyed during the laſt ſummer of his: this certainly would ſecure to them a great name. The generals, miniſters,

ambaſſadors,

ambaſſadors, and private ſecretaries of his Pruſſian majeſty, well know that the ſpirit of this prince was diſcernible in every thing which he did in the ſummer of 1786; and what Mr. Hertzberg, the miniſter, ſaid on this ſubject, has certainly more weight than the idle reports of all Germany. I ſaw Frederic at many moments when he appeared to me capable of deciding reſpecting a war; and though he could not have taken the field in perſon, one might read in his eyes that his head was ſufficiently clear to form the beſt plans, and to direct the execution of them with perfect propriety. A few days before my arrival at Potſdam, he wrote, with his own hand, inſtructions to his ambaſſador at one of the moſt powerful courts in Europe, which, as I was aſſured, were a maſter-piece of politics. I learned alſo that, during my reſidence there, he had formed reſolutions reſpecting a foreign affair, which were as bold and deciſive as any he had ever formed at the uſual age of vivacity and vigour.

My readers will, perhaps, wiſh to know in what manner his majeſty ſpent his time during the ſeventeen days I reſided at Potſdam. His manner of living, from the period of my departure till his death, may be ſeen in the Memoirs of Mr. Hertzberg.

After his majesty's disorder had become so serious, he began business at a very early hour. Before that period, the cabinet secretaries never made their appearance till towards six or seven in the morning; but after it he always required their attendance at four. "My condition" (these are the memorable words by which his majesty announced to his secretaries this change) "obliges me to give you this trouble, which will not continue long. As my life is on the decline, I must turn to advantage that part of it which remains, for it does not belong to me but to the state."—What a lesson to future kings, princes, and rulers! for every one knows that there is no king or prince, great or small, who has not occasion for his time. Every morning at four, after Frederic had given audience to his adjutant, one of his hussars in waiting brought him all the reports of his ministers and generals, all the dispatches of his ambassadors, and all the letters which had arrived in the night at Berlin, from different countries. Having examined them, and selected such as were of most immediate consequence, he placed on one side those which he wished to read himself, and on the other those which he intended his cabinet secretaries should give him an account of. His

secretaries

ſecretaries were then called, who were obliged to come from *Sans-Souci* to Potſdam by four in the morning. When they arrived, his majeſty delivered to them ſuch papers as he wiſhed them to read; they then repaired to an apartment without the caſtle, read the whole, and made ſhort extracts from them: in the mean time his majeſty peruſed all his letters; after which the ſecretaries were called in ſucceſſion, each having his pen in his hand. Frederic firſt dictated what concerned the letters which he had read himſelf; his ſecretaries then gave an account of thoſe from which they had made extracts; and his majeſty dictated to them his orders, and the anſwers he meant to give, almoſt word for word. Thus, in general, from the hour of four to ſix or ſeven in the morning, one ſick mortal ruled a whole kingdom, and diſpatched at the ſame time all foreign affairs. The cabinet ſecretaries then returned to Potſdam, wrote out fair copies of what the king had dictated to them, and brought them after dinner to be ſigned. But, what is rarely done in the adminiſtration of ſtates, his majeſty read over again all theſe letters and orders, before he put his ſignature to them.

Frederic then, after ſeven in the morning, might have given himſelf up to indolence, and been exposed to languor, if he had thought proper; but this he never could nor would do. Such a mode of life no sovereign can follow.

At that hour the bill of fare was brought him, but only for dinner, as he never supped; at the same hour all the productions of his gardens and green-houses, which had appeared since the preceding day, were also brought him. I always saw them in large baskets placed on the tables of the anti-chamber; they were the choicest and most beautiful of his fruits, consisting of cherries, grapes, melons, peaches, apricots, plums, and *pisangs** ; and care was taken not to suffer a single cherry to be amongst them that was deformed by the smallest speck. Frederic in general ate some of these fruits.

At eight, when I arrived, he was almost always employed in reading, either a French translation of some ancient author, or some work respecting modern history; but as his hand was so weak that he could not hold a moderate octavo volume, he had every work of a large size formed into small divisions of a few sheets each. From the hour of eight I remained with him as long as he thought proper; generally half an hour, but sometimes a whole hour. After

* A beautiful kind of figs brought from the island of Java. T.

my departure the commandant of Potſdam, the worthy, honeſt, and mild lieutenant-general De Rohdich, arrived to receive the orders of the day; but this was always a momentary buſineſs, becauſe at four in the morning an officer gave an account of every thing that had paſſed at the gates of Potſdam, and in the whole garriſon. Between nine and eleven his majeſty gave audience to the adjutants, and other officers with whom he had occaſion to ſpeak.

At eleven, count de Lucheſini and general Goertz, his majeſty's uſual company at table, made their appearance. From the time of my arrival till near that of my departure, count de Schwerin, firſt equerry—and after my departure, till his majeſty's death, Mr. Hertzberg the miniſter, and count Pinto a Piedmonteſe, and colonel of engineers, were generally of the party alſo. Beſides theſe, he had with him ſometimes one of his generals, and ſometimes one of his majors. It is to be obſerved that Frederic ſent an invitation every morning even to thoſe who were admitted to his table the whole year round.

The dinner laſted ſometimes only half an hour, but oftener an hour and a half. The king ate always with a keen appetite, and for the moſt part too much. He drank a kind of white wine, made at Bergerac in France, but with great moderation. When dinner was over, he always flept more or lefs, but never long; after which he took a few difhes of coffee, then fat in the fun, on his terrace, or amufed himfelf with fome object or other. For example, he had always fomething to do with jewellers and lapidaries. One day, while I was with him, he reviewed all his jewels and precious ftones, which were very numerous. Thofe in his own apartment were eftimated at five millions of crowns*.

I had generally orders to wait upon his majefty at three in the afternoon; but my vifit was often delayed half an hour or more, on account of his being bufy, or afleep. The audience lafted as long as that of the morning. His majefty's occupations then recommenced, and various letters were brought him to be figned. One day I faw count de Finkenftein enter;

* Precious ftones excited a kind of paffion in the capricious mind of Frederic. His tafte in this refpect was fingular: brilliants he confidered as not fufficiently beautiful. He had always before him, befides a leaden cheft full of fnuff, two other wooden chefts, and four fnuff-boxes of Silefian agate. They were ornamented with precious ftones of all colours, which were neither fapphires, rubies, nor emeralds, as I at firft imagined; but real brilliants, with foils of different colours placed under them, according to his majefty's directions.

and

and at the ſame time prince Dolgoroucky, the Ruſſian envoy, had his audience of leave. Often, as I was going out, officers and engineers were entering with plans, drawings, &c.

The king's evening party arrived at half after five, and conſiſted uſually of the chamberlain, count de Lucheſini, and general Goertz. During the whole time I reſided at Potſdam, and even during the time he himſelf reſided there, count Schwerin, the grand equerry, was admitted alſo. Two days after my departure, he was ſucceeded by Mr. de Hertzberg, who, as well as count de Schwerin, attended the king, and remained at *Sans-Souci* till the period of his death. The king always converſed cheerfully with this ſociety, who afterwards ſupped together by themſelves; and Frederic made a young man from Berlin read to him, ſometimes Cicero, ſometimes Plutarch, and ſometimes Voltaire, till the hour of ten, at which he uſually went to ſleep.

The king therefore, during his laſt illneſs, that is to ſay, for the ſpace of nine months, ſpent all his evenings with count Lucheſini and count Goertz, who compoſed the whole company when there were none of the miniſters of Berlin at *Sans-Souci*. For the ſix preceding years, he had ſpent them, except on extraordi-

nary

nary occaſions, in a *tête à tête* with count de Lucheſini; but when his majeſty's oppreſſion increaſed, after the review of Sileſia, in 1785, he admitted, as a third, count Goertz, as he could no longer ſupport a converſation with Lucheſini alone, who was for ſix years in his majeſty's company every day, and for five years his only companion in the evening. No philoſopher, therefore, or man of letters, was better acquainted with the character of Frederic the Great, than this learned, amiable, and lively Italian. The king not only employed him often in foreign affairs, and ſecret commiſſions, but, from what the reigning prince of Deſſau aſſured me, entruſted him with all his ſecrets; ſo that he knows the internal affairs of Pruſſia, as well as thoſe of foreign countries, reſpecting which he was perfectly inſtructed by his late majeſty. The worthy prince of Deſſau told me, that the preſent king, on his acceſſion to the throne, addreſſed the following compliment to the count: "You was the late king's beſt "friend; be the ſame to me alſo." Lucheſini was properly his majeſty's *literary friend.* Frederic no longer read new books with any pleaſure; it is well known that he never read any book in German except the Bible, and *True Chriſtianity by Arndts*, the only two works which the king his father suffered him to have when in prison at Küstrin. Luchesini, however, read every thing; for he was well versed in the German, and consequently could give the king an account of every novelty in the German literature, with as much facility as he could make him acquainted with those of other nations.

Man always wishes to commit certain thoughts and sentiments to some friend, in order that he may unburden his mind. Many princes choose for confidants their valets or game-keepers; but Frederic the Great had good sense enough to choose Luchesini. He was, above all, his confidant respecting his literary works: the king gave him all his manuscripts to read, and conversed with him on the subject of them. No one therefore would be fitter to publish his majesty's works, as he could enrich them with notes and illustrations received from Frederic's own mouth. Luchesini, who forgets nothing, is on this account richer and more abundant in anecdotes than any person is or could be. Had he been the historian of this modern Cæsar, as he must at least know the literary history of all his works, the public would have set a higher value on many little pieces, which at present appear uninteresting, because we are not acquainted with the circumstances ſtancesthatgaveriſeto them, and which Luchefini muſt have been informed of by his majeſty himſelf. But all this will die with him, unleſs he executes what I have earneſtly requeſted, and here again requeſt him to do, in the name of the whole world and of poſterity.

Count Luchefini is at preſent thirty-two years of age; and the greatneſs of his character, his candour, probity, integrity, love of truth, prudence, fidelity, deep penetration, prodigious memory, erudition, and profound philoſophical and political genius, convince me that he is fully qualified to execute what I expect from him, and which no perſon living can do ſo well. By this he would merit the gratitude of poſterity, and undoubtedly acquire immortal glory. I ſaw in his houſe at Potſdam a ſtriking proof of the confidence which the king had in his diſcretion. Having aſked him what was become of his majeſty's correſpondence with d'Alembert, "The miniſter of France," ſaid he, "imagines that the whole of this correſpondence has been ſacrificed to Vulcan. The day when that learned man died, Mr. de Vergennes, the miniſter of ſtate, haſtened to his houſe, and demanded, by order of the king of France, all the king of Pruſſia's letters to him. The letters were accordingly delivered to the miniſter, who immediately

immediately committed them to the flames. But notwithstanding this precaution," continued Luchesini, " this correspondence is not destroyed, as the French minister believes; for though all the letters were written by the king's own hand, they were, in compliance with his majesty's desire, all copied by Mr. Cat: Frederic sent only copies to d'Alembert, and preserved the originals." To convince me that this was true, Luchesini opened his bureau; and shewing me six large packets, said, " These are the king's letters to d'Alembert:" they undoubtedly amounted to some hundreds. The late king's answers exist also. " You know his majesty's writing," added Luchesini: " I will open some of the letters, as chance directs, and you will plainly see that they are originals." One of the letters he read, and afterwards put it into my hands. One part of it related to literary, philosophical, and theological objects; and the other contained sarcasms on the politics of the time: the whole was written in a bold and decisive strain. Few of the French literati, philosophers, and above all theologians, and ministers of state, could read these letters, which according to every appearance will never be published, without being affected in the most sensible manner. From what my intimacy

timacy with count Luchesini gave me an opportunity of knowing, I am of opinion that they will never be all printed.—The second question I asked him was, whether it was true that the king had written the history of the war of seven years; that through the stupidity of a page it had been one day burnt; and that the king said nothing else to the page, who threw himself on his knees when he informed his majesty of the misfortune, than these words—"So I must "write this history again?" Luchesini assured me that this anecdote was true; and that Frederic had really written a second time the history of the war of seven years.

A heroi-comic poem, in the style of the *Maid of Orleans*, the subject and design of which I neither should nor will mention; and which, as I have been told, will perhaps be published, was intended to be so several years ago. Schmid, the celebrated engraver of Berlin, had executed the plates with which it was to be ornamented; but the king having changed his mind, the poem was suppressed, and the plates were burnt. Counsellor Brandes of Hanover, who has in his collection the finest books and prints that the world ever produced, is now in possession of these engravings.

Another heroi-comic poem, on the partition of

of Poland, in the ſtyle alſo of the *Maid of Orleans*, which the king had no intention of printing, and which probably never will be printed, was found ſome years ago, very much to the king's ſorrow, in the preſs at Hamburgh: a well-known bookſeller had advertiſed it, and even quoted ſome paſſages from it. This came to the knowledge of Lucheſini, who was much ſurpriſed when he ſaw the extracts copied, word for word, from the king's manuſcript; and he haſtened to inform his majeſty of this ſingular circumſtance. Frederic was as much aſtoniſhed as Lucheſini; for he had entruſted the manuſcript only to Voltaire and another perſon. "What is to be done in this conjuncture?" ſaid the king. Lucheſini replied, "Send as ſoon as poſſible a courier to Hamburgh, to order the Pruſſian reſident to go inſtantly to the bookſeller, and to demand, with threats of vengeance in caſe of a refuſal, the manuſcript, and all the ſheets that have been printed: then reward the bookſeller in a manner worthy of a king." This plan, which pleaſed Frederic, was punctually and ſucceſsfully executed, after four ſheets had been already printed. I was told by ſome perſon at Hanover, that Voltaire had ſtolen this poem from Frederic, and, cauſing it to be copied, appropriated it to himſelf; and that Beau-

marchais

marchais had bought the manuſcript of Voltaire's executors, and ſold it at Hamburgh.

Frederic, at an early period of life, ſpoke the French language, and employed it when he wrote in preference to any other. He was therefore, during his whole life, fond of the French literature, and compoſed all his works in French. But it may be aſked, why did he not pay attention to the light which Gotſched, and ſeveral profeſſors at Leipſic, diffuſed abroad, throughout all Germany, after the year 1740? I ſhall reply, becauſe he was too modeſt; for though he had got far before the whole ſecond half of the eighteenth century, he however conſidered himſelf ſo deficient in thoſe kinds of literary objects, that he never looked from *Sans-Souci* to Leipſic; and, with regard to what concerns the empire of faſhion, he was great enough to emancipate himſelf from it, and he always remained voluntarily behind his age in this reſpect. His army, till the time of his death, was dreſſed in the ſame manner as they were when he mounted the throne. He even neglected very neceſſary alterations, which his ſucceſſor was obliged to make; and he neglected them merely becauſe they were alterations. In conſequence of this mode of thinking, the clothes of his footmen and chaſſeurs were cut in the ſame ſtyle in

1786 as they had been in 1740. His ſtrict adherence to theſe minutiæ was agreeable to the firmneſs of his mind and character; and this was the true reaſon why he ſet little value on the German literature. He did not, however, deſpiſe the German muſes: on the contrary, he never diſputed that rank which they deſerved and held; and he was contented with not cultivating them himſelf. During his youth, we had no German Voltaire; our geniuſes were not then born; and on this account Frederic applied to the French literature, which in the beginning of the reign of Louis XIV. was as flouriſhing and as far advanced as the German literature is at preſent, a hundred years later: for this reaſon Frederic never read any German book. His taſte for foreign literature, and above all for the French, was ſtrengthened, on the other hand, by his intimate and daily intercourſe with Algarotti, Voltaire, and D'Argens. For ſome time after the two firſt wars of Sileſia, he had theſe celebrated men always with him; and that was the happieſt and moſt tranquil period of his reign. The pleaſure and charms of their company ſurpaſſed every thing that he ſaw, heard, or knew of the ſpirit of the ſociety of the German literati. Sulzer loved and reſpected the Germans; but he however allowed

 that

that many of them, being unacquainted with the world, would have been greatly embarraſſed in the marble hall of *Sans-Souci*, if ſeated at table with the king, Voltaire, Algarotti, and D'Argens; and that ſuch a ſituation would rather have given them a colic, than inſpired them with wit. Sulzer has often aſſured me that it was a thouſand times more agreeable and more delightful to hear Voltaire, Algarotti, and D'Argens converſe together, than to read the beſt written and moſt amuſing book. This candid philoſopher, this good patriot, therefore, was not aſtoniſhed that a German literary man, dull and aukward in every thing which he ſaid or did, ſhould appear to the king very ſtupid, in compariſon of thoſe lively and brilliant geniuſes. He aſſured me that the king conſidered a German wit as a being abſolutely imaginary; and though the number of geniuſes increaſed every day in that country, none of them were ever ſeen in the marble hall of *Sans-Souci*. But it was frequented by a Voltaire, an Algarotti, and a D'Argens; and their ſuppers in the marble hall of the caſtle of *Sans-Souci*, ſo juſtly called the abode of peace, happineſs, domeſtic eaſe, genius, and the muſes, continued ſo long, that the ſervants who waited at table contracted ſwellings in their legs. At thoſe nocturnal

feſtivals

feſtivals of wit and the muſes, the company drank champagne. There is undoubtedly no place in Germany where ſo much wit was ever diſplayed, as in the marble hall of *Sans-Souci*. This I often repeated to myſelf, when ſeated between the Corinthian pillars oppoſite to the *Venus Urania*, and the Apollo, who holds in his hand Lucretius, in which is written, in large gold characters—

> Te ſociam ſtudeo ſcribundis verſibus eſſe,
> Quos ego de rerum naturâ pangere conor.

Frederic did not deſpiſe the Germans, though he never invited any of their literary men to dinner. All his grand enterprizes were executed by Germans; and it was with their aſſiſtance that he ſignalized himſelf by ſo many bold and immortal actions: neither did he deſpiſe the German language; for he required that all letters ſent to him on the foreign affairs of his kingdom, all the reports of his miniſters and generals, and every thing that concerned the whole army, ſhould be written in German. The Academy of Sciences at Berlin alone was obliged to write to him in French; and he always returned an anſwer in the ſame language. All this was eſtabliſhed, and continued the ſame, from the beginning of his reign to the cloſe of it. He himſelf dreſſed in 1786 exactly in the ſame manner as he dreſſed in 1740. His whole wardrobe, which I have ſeen, except two ſurtouts —that which he wore, and another—conſiſted in two ſuits of uniforms, one for ſummer, and the other for winter. The ſurtout which he never wore, was of ſky-blue ſattin, embroidered in gold by his ſiſter, the ducheſs dowager of Brunſwic. He never put it on, becauſe he conſidered it as too gaudy.

Though Frederic read only French books, and ſet a higher eſteem on Voltaire than on Gotſched, he was no leſs great and good, at all times, in every thing which he did; and, notwithſtanding this, his goodneſs was doubted even till the moment of his death. Count de Mirabeau was not aſhamed to ſay, in his famous Letter to Frederic William II. "Frederic merited the admiration, but never the "love, of mankind."—The king's behaviour to me, and many expreſſions which I heard from his mouth, prove the goodneſs of his heart; for, without this valuable quality, he would not have ſhewn himſelf ſo friendly and grateful towards me. One day, when I had the good fortune to conſole him in a moment of dejection, had he not poſſeſſed real goodneſs of heart, he would not have ſaid—"I never receive greater "pleaſure than when I can cauſe a houſe to "be

"be built for a poor man. Nothing in life
"ever gave me greater pain, than when I ſaw
"my poor ſoldiers, who had expoſed their lives
"for their country, neglected when ſick or
"wounded; nothing ever afflicted me more
"than when I have found myſelf the innocent
"cauſe of the death of any perſon whatever."
It appears to me that, if any ever exiſted, theſe are traits of humanity, and of a noble and feeling heart.—Haller ſeems as if deſirous of inſinuating, in the third book of his *Uſong*, that, according to Frederic, there was no difference between right and wrong, and that this great man placed vice above virtue: yet the moſt certain and beſt authenticated anecdotes of the life of my hero plainly ſhew, that he poſſeſſed the moſt amiable qualities—goodneſs of heart, mildneſs, a diſpoſition to attend always to the different ſituations of mankind; in ſhort, benevolence, ſenſibility, and the moſt paternal tenderneſs towards his ſubjects. When his father, who was far from treating him as a good father ought to treat a ſon, ſent for him to his bed-ſide, in the laſt moments of his life, he was ſeen to quit the apartment in tears, very much affected, and oppreſſed with grief. Tears, in this ſituation, indicate quite another thing than the tears which are generally ſhed.—But

let us read only his affecting and interesting correspondence with Suhm; or the charming and friendly letters which he wrote, during the war of seven years, to the old countess of Camas; and we will then see whether it is possible to doubt respecting the character of the hereditary prince, and that of the king. His constitution was not robust; and the weakness of his nerves, and some excesses in youth, had brought many complaints upon him at a very early period of life. When very young, he had exhausted and enervated himself by women; and, the year before his accession to the throne, he confessed to Suhm that he was become impotent. My unhappy experience, says he, in one of his letters to that gentleman, has made me a physician. But who ever knew better than Frederic how to harden and strengthen his body by the effects of character and disposition?

This weakness was a subject of triumph to the French, in the beginning of the war of seven years, a little before the battle of Rosbach. "With the marquis of Brandenburg* "we hope to have soon done," said they; "for how

* This was the title which the French lieutenants and ensigns gave to Frederic the Great.

" can

"can an impotent king make war upon *us?*" In certain respects the French were much in the right: for a man who is in this situation may be a wit, and good-humoured; but he rarely possesses true genius, or energy and strength of mind. The French, for this very reason, thought themselves so certain, before the battle of Rosbach, of realising their ideas, that they openly boasted at Versailles that they would soon bring the king of Prussia prisoner to Paris. A lady, to whom this was told, replied—"So much "the better; I shall at least have the pleasure of "seeing a king." At the same time there appeared an epigram on Frederic, ascribed to a lady, in which it was said that he was the greatest of heroes and of kings; but the author added, "Alas! what a pity that *he is not a man!*"

He was naturally weak; and yet, when he was only hereditary prince, he was decidedly a philosopher. The trifling and apish tricks of the military art, which his father was fond of, and which are the delight of so many princes, gave him great disgust. His father having employed a whole day, from morning till night, in reviewing his troops, and making them march from right to left, and from left to right, he wrote to Suhm, "We kill ourselves here with "performing exercise; and lose in folly that

" valuable time which can never be recover-ed." In another letter to Suhm, he calls all this military vanity " the real amusement of children." Amidst his father's reviews, he sighed after his books, his vines, his melons, and his cherries; but his studies afforded him the greatest pleasure. When prince royal, he was niggardly of nothing but his time; and he always sowed for futurity. He could not comprehend, however elegant he might be at that period, how people could speak of fashions, dress, and other objects relating to women; how they could seriously occupy their thoughts with such trifles—expose themselves continually to misery, and yet fear death. The life of a courtier appeared to him to be no life at all.

The victories of Munich over the Turks, however, agitated and disturbed his mind, amidst all the tranquillity of his philosophy. It appears to me that this inquietude excited that ardour for the glory of arms, which afterwards glowed so warmly in the bosom of Frederic. But this ardour soon appeared to be extinguished. On the 26th of November 1737, he wrote to Suhm—" Do not talk to me, dear Suhm, of " heroic dispositions, except with regard to " friendship. If goodness of heart, fidelity, and " humanity are as necessary as the ferocious rage " of

" of the warrior and conqueror; if a proper " choice of men, who may be useful to us, can " supply the want of that great strength of " mind which forms vast projects; and if " mildness and good intentions are of more " worth than that irresistible activity of men " who seem born to overturn the whole world— " in that case I aspire at being a hero, but un- " der these conditions only. Benevolence and " mildness form a good citizen, but not a great " man: for this reason I am not so vain as to " seek for a great name; I choose rather to be " only a man, since I cannot be so unless I do " all the good that the situation in which I am " will permit."—Such were the sentiments which Frederic entertained three years before he mounted the throne. The people of Berlin, however, were not acquainted with his greatness. They were told that he gave elegant entertainments at Rheinsberg; that he was fond of women and music; that he had a neat foot, and danced elegantly: and all Berlin promised themselves, under his reign, golden days, continual festivals, plays, operas, and balls.

This was not altogether the idea of Frederic William his father, when he said on his death-bed to the queen his spouse—" Well, you " are going to rejoice at my death. At pre-

" sent

“ ſent the people of Berlin are going to amuſe “ themſelves; but remember what I ſay—in “ the end matters will be quite different.”—Frederic was not born a warrior; but he was the boldeſt warrior and the firſt general of his age, becauſe he was forced and wiſhed to be ſo. Notwithſtanding his propenſity to effeminacy, he diſpenſed with the moſt requiſite conveniences of life, and thoſe which few people can renounce. When king, he never uſed a morning gown, night-cap, or ſlippers. In bed, he always ſlept with his hat on. One day, ſeeing me cold, he complained of the ſeverity of the climate of Germany, and added that he had always found cold and dampneſs very diſagreeable to him. Nevertheleſs he brought on his laſt illneſs by his own imprudence; for during the two laſt grand operations in Sileſia, in the year 1785, he uſed to remain from morning till night without a cloak or great coat, before his army, expoſed to cold, and very heavy rains; and afterwards to dine, without changing his wet clothes, in an open barn, with his generals, and foreigners from various countries.

Frederic poſſeſſed a vigour and activity of mind which were almoſt above human; and on this account he often required from his generals, ministers, soldiers, and physicians, things far above the usual powers of man.

It has been often said, by French as well as German officers, that Frederic had as good engineers, and as good officers of artillery, in his army, as any other sovereign. But he always expected that they should perform wonders, with little money; and though the Prussians understood sieges very badly, he never employed above half of what was necessary for carrying one on. At the siege of Prague, in 1757, he had not in the space of thirty miles round a single cannon of large bore. The garrison of Olmutz, in 1758, was twice as numerous as the Prussian army who besieged it; and the city had two communications open with the Austrian army: but his vast genius undertook every enterprize with a half, or even fourth part, of the forces necessary; and yet he always succeeded. How great would his joy be, did he know that the duke of Brunswic took, in Holland, batteries and fortresses with a handful of *cuirassiers*; and vessels armed with cannon by the help of a few hussars!

Notwithstanding his superior genius and courage, the private life of the philosopher of *Sans-Souci* was always calm and simple; and, in that retreat where he was not obliged to act the hero and the king, he loved to act the man.

In

In muſic, in painting, and even in the colour of his furniture, he loved every thing pleaſing and ſoft. His taſte for painting, in the grand Roman ſtyle, was not fixed till the latter part of his life; but he had always an averſion to the terrible of that art, which he thought was invented for executioners. One day when a young girl attempted to drown herſelf below his windows at Potſdam, he called out for aſſiſtance, with every ſign of the utmoſt terror and diſtreſs.

But Frederic ſhewed very few ſentiments of mildneſs, when the two thirds of Europe took up arms againſt him, and threatened his deſtruction. He did not preſerve the honour of his family, or the immortality of his name; and at a time when he thought every thing loſt, he did not procure ſafety by mildneſs and ſoft words. When a lion is ſeverely wounded, he never preſents his paw, in a friendly manner, to his perſecutors. Sophiſts may ſay that the enlightened beneficence which organizes and vivifies empires, has never yet appeared upon thrones, pure and without mixture. Cold and harſh politicians may deſpiſe the millions of crowns which Frederic, after the war of ſeven years, diſtributed among his ſubjects; they may ſay, as long as they chooſe, that he gave with one hand, to plunder doubly with the other.

But

But whatever they may ſay in this reſpect will be an abſurdity; for Frederic certainly never expected large intereſt for thoſe ſums which he diſtributed among his ſubjects who had ſuffered by fires or inundations.

Of all that the pen of a celebrated miniſter, who poſſeſſes great genius, has tranſmitted on this ſubject to poſterity—of all that hiſtorians may ſay in their immortal works—and of all that a great French warrior * has remarked—nothing can elevate or touch the ſoul ſo much as the two following anecdotes, which diſplay great humanity and magnanimity, and which in my opinion are the moſt authentic proofs of the king's greatneſs of mind. Theſe anecdotes were related to me by one of thoſe men for whom I entertain the greateſt eſteem and reſpect—lieutenant general Stamford, at preſent chamberlain to the Stadtholder, and preceptor to the two Princes of Orange. I ſhall relate them here, though they may have been printed already.

One day, whilethe king was alone in his apartment at *Sans-Souci*, he happened to fall aſleep. Before the window, which was open, ſtood a box containing a large quantity of ducats,

* Count de Guibert, in his Elogium on the King of Pruſſia: London (Paris), 1787.

rolled

rolled up in different pieces of paper. One of his laquais, who chanced to paſs the window at that time, ſeeing the king aſleep, took a roll of the ducats without any ceremony, and walked off with it. Frederic, however, ſoon diſcovered that he had been robbed; and calling one of his huſſars in waiting, ſaid to him, "I have "loſt a roll of ducats, and I deſire to know "who has taken it." The huſſar, in great conſternation, aſſured the king that he knew nothing at all of the matter; adding, that his majeſty perhaps laboured under a miſtake, and that it ſeemed impoſſible that any one could take his ducats in his preſence. "If you cannot," replied the king, "tell me the name of the thief, "I will make you reſponſible for the robbery." The poor huſſar, frightened almoſt to death, repreſented to his majeſty that he could not anſwer for what paſſed in his apartment when he was not there. "I am not unjuſt," ſaid Frederic; "but as you are well acquainted with your "comrades, you muſt know whether there be a "thief amongſt them." The huſſar inſtantly retired, made every enquiry poſſible to diſcover the guilty perſon, and at length ſucceeded. As ſoon as he was brought before his majeſty, he addreſſed him in the following words: "You villain! you have robbed me of a roll of "ducats.

"ducats. Hold—here is another roll, of the "ſame value; quit the palace this moment, "and get out my territories as faſt as you can: "loſe not a ſingle moment; for if you remain "here long you will infallibly be hanged."

Another huſſar had robbed him, at different times, of ſums to the amount of twenty thouſand crowns; and had, beſides, accepted preſents from ſeveral of the foreign miniſters reſident at Berlin, for communicating to them every thing that he heard and ſaw. The king, being informed of this perfidy, ſent for the huſſar, reproached him with his crime, and ſaid, "You "have robbed and deceived me; as a puniſhment "for your ill conduct, I make you a drummer." His majeſty then called an adjutant, and immediately gave orders for his being made a drummer. The huſſar retired with the adjutant, went into his apartment under pretence of fetching ſomething, and ſhot himſelf through the head. When the adjutant told the king what had happened, he appeared very much affected, and exclaimed—"My God! tell me, then, did I treat this man too harſhly?

After ſuch traits as theſe, Frederic undoubtedly well merited to be ſtyled the Solomon of the North. Veſtris the dancer ſaid therefore, at Paris, that there were only three great men

In the world—the king of Pruſſia, Voltaire, and himſelf. Veſtris was a fool, and the cauſtic Voltaire an impertinent fellow. It is well known that the latter had the impudence to ſay, that he gave Frederic the nick-name of the Solomon of the North, and that he had always retained it. But there are ſome mihds who find poiſon every where; who take delight in collecting it, and then diffuſing it abroad in epigrams.

It will perhaps not appear altogether out of ſeaſon, if I ſay a few words here reſpecting the king's dogs, for even allowing that he carried his fondneſs for them too far, it is at leaſt one proof more, to be added to a great many others, of his warmth and goodneſs of heart. Amongſt mankind he never found the ſame fidelity and attachment as amongſt thoſe animals; and it is probably for this reaſon that he loved them ſo much. I always ſaw two of them in his apartment; they were greyhounds, of the ſmall Italian ſpecies; and one of them always lay on a chair, covered with blue ſattin, cloſe to the king, while the other occupied a large couch made of the ſame ſtuff. They ſeldom ſtirred, and never barked when I entered. When Frederic made himſelf be carried to the terrace, to enjoy the ſun, a chair was always placed

placed at his side for one of these greyhounds. No stranger could then approach the terrace without being announced by the dogs. Frederic, who loved solitude and repose above all things, could no longer bear any stranger whom he had not invited to approach his hermitage, nor to see him even at a distance.

In 1785, when he was at the review of Silesia for the last time, one of his dogs being sick, he gave orders that a courier should be sent every day to bring him an account of its situation. On his return, finding that the little animal was dead and buried, he caused it to be taken from the earth, that he might have the pleasure of seeing it once more; shut himself up the whole day, and cried for it like a child.—Stamford is my authority also for this anecdote.

No one can deny that goodness of heart, with all its attending circumstances and mild effects, always occasions our chief happiness in this world. Without goodness of heart, genius, wit, and the most brilliant abilities, will never secure us perfect enjoyment. Of the truth of this no one was more firmly persuaded than Frederic the Great. The inhabitants of Berlin preserve the remembrance of a great many instances of goodness in this celebrated prince—instances worthy of a celestial soul; and which being imprinted in the minds of his ſubjects, and repeated from mouth to mouth, will be tranſmitted to poſterity.

But when any one was ſo impertinent as to approach him with any inſipid play upon words, or affected wit, he indeed was no longer found mild, patient, and affable. He well knew how to diſmiſs ſuch people very drily, or to turn his back upon them without the leaſt ceremony.

Frederic often complained, eſpecially during the latter part of his life, of being haraſſed with impertinence from ſtrangers; and very often from young Frenchmen, who, as I was told by count de Lucheſini, ſurpaſſed in this reſpect any thing that can be imagined. The king ſaid, one evening, to Lucheſini: "Having aſked " a French officer, who was this day preſented to " me, what regiment he belonged to; Sire, re- " plied he, to the regiment of *Rouiſſilon*, otherwiſe " called *Trouſſe-cotillon*. Your ſervant, Sir, ſaid I; " and immediately turning on my heel, left the " fool to meditate on his ſtupidity."—He deteſted cringing, and thoſe compliments which people at courts are generally ſo laviſh of: he loved openneſs, boldneſs, and loyalty in every thing; but nothing pleaſed him more than honeſty. Though he often carried his goodneſs and condeſcenſion a

little

little too far perhaps, he never loſt ſight of his dignity, even in the ſimpleſt parts of etiquette.

Two of the Pope's chamberlains having requeſted, by general Lentulus, an audience of his majeſty, he complied, and appointed a time when he would receive them. Lentulus miſunderſtanding the king, or chooſing to be more polite than his maſter, added, that his majeſty wiſhed that the chamberlains ſhould be conducted to the palace in his own carriage. Many people, indeed, had ſome of the king's carriages at their command: I myſelf had one during the whole time I ſtaid at Potſdam; but it was only a carriage from his majeſty's ſtables, as ugly as a common hack, and drawn by two horſes, which, as I ſometimes carried my wife with me, ſtuck a long time one day in the ſands, at the diſtance of half a league from Potſdam.—His majeſty never intended that theſe gentlemen ſhould be brought in one of his coaches; but as the domeſtic who received the orders of Lentulus comprehended the general as badly as the general had comprehended the king, ſix beautiful horſes were put to one of the fineſt of the royal coaches, and in this manner the chamberlains were conveyed towards Potſdam. The king, who happened to be at the window, ſeeing the two Italians advancing in triumph, aſked who they were; and being told that they were the Pope's chamberlains, he fell into a violent passion at this mistake; ordered the coach to be immediately sent away, and a hack to be brought to carry the chamberlains back to their lodgings. When the chamberlains came forth from the palace, they were in the utmost astonishment; and having asked one of the king's domestics why their equipage was changed, he replied, with great coolness, that it was a piece of ancient etiquette in the court of Prussia, that persons of their rank should be conducted to an audience in a splendid carriage, and sent back in a common hackney coach.

I might here mention many of Frederic's epigrams and sarcasms; and I should certainly have published them, had I alone been the object against which they were directed; but he employed them against princes, literary men, and great lords. Princes and lords might easily have endured them; but they would have hurt men of letters, whose existence often depends on the opinion entertained of them. He often bore with patience, and good-nature, very bold answers; but he could never suffer affected witticisms: the conversation at his table was however, for the most part, lively and entertaining.

The converſation having one day fallen on the fondneſs which phyſicians formerly ſhewed for treating their patients in ſuch a manner that they almoſt ſtifled them in their apartments, his majeſty related the following anecdote :— The emperor Leopold being once ſeized with a violent fever, was ſhut up in his chamber in ſuch a manner, that the ſmalleſt ray of light could not find admiſſion. His phyſician arriving one morning, had a good deal of difficulty to find the bed; and when he had at laſt ſucceeded, he was ſtill embarraſſed to find the emperor's arm. He felt all over the bed and bed-clothes; while the emperor, who was a very grave man, never ſaid a ſingle word : and after a good deal of labour, thinking that he had gained his point, and got hold of his majeſty's arm, he began with great compoſure to count the beats of his pulſe. But the emperor, much ſurpriſed at the incredible miſtake into which the phyſician had fallen, undeceived his ſimplicity, by ſaying, in a very pathetic tone of voice,

Hoc eſt membrum noſtrum imperiale, ſacrocæſareum.

One of the ſevereſt ſarcaſms Frederic ever uttered was addreſſed to the French ambaſſador (the marquis de Valori, if I am not miſtaken) in the opera-houſe at Berlin. All the actors were ready upon the ſtage; and when the ſervants attempted to draw up the curtain, it was prevented by ſome obſtacle from riſing any higher than juſt to ſhew the legs of the performers: upon which the king cried out from his box—"Monſieur de Valori! Monſieur de "Valori," addreſſing himſelf to the ambaſſador, "you now ſee the French government—many legs and no heads."

His majeſty being much diſpleaſed with a windmill ſituated above his orangery at *Sans-Souci*, ſent word to the proprietor, that, if he would reſign his right to it, he would make him a preſent in money, and give him three mills in another place. The miller replied very drily, that his mill had for a long time maintained him and his children; that it ſtood on a ſpot from which he enjoyed a beautiful proſpect; and that he was reſolved to live and die in his mill. The king was ſatisfied with this anſwer, and the man retained his mill. Some time after, Frederic walking with one of his favourites in the gardens of *Sans-Souci*, looked towards the mill, and ſaid he was extremely ſorry that the miller would not part with it. The favourite, well-knowing how fond the king was of accompliſhing his ends by money, had the boldneſs to reply, that his majeſty had nothing

thing to do but to gild it. To this obſervation the king returned no anſwer. He however laughed very heartily one day at the anſwer of a Dutch architect, whom he called an aſs—" I " muſt indeed," ſaid the architect, " be an aſs, " to bear all the burden which your majeſty is " pleaſed to lay upon me."

There were formerly within the circumference of Berlin ſeveral fields and meadows; and, if I am not miſtaken, the proprietors had the right of hunting in them. The king ſaid one day to Mr. De la Touche, the French ambaſſador, that, on comparing the plans of Berlin and Paris, it appeared to him that the former of theſe cities was as large as the latter. The ambaſſador's reply made the king laugh heartily—" That is true, pleaſe your majeſty; " but we never reap in Paris."

Frederic had in Baron de Munchauſen an excellent miniſter of ſtate. I often had the happineſs of ſeeing this extraordinary man at his houſe in Berlin. To great penetration he united deep learning, integrity, proof againſt every attack, and a firmneſs of character which made him often contradict Frederic; but nevertheleſs Munchauſen died in the miniſtry. The king once imagined that Munchauſen had rejected a donation of the abbey of Kloſterberguen from an in-

inclination towards pietifm. This fufpicion was very unjuft: Munchaufen was a man of enlightened piety, but not an enthufiaft. The king one day at table told him his fufpicion, and tormented him a long time by pleafantries, to which Munchaufen replied with much drynefs, and in a very laconic manner. The king at length faid, "Munchaufen perhaps is a Moravian." "No," anfwered Munchaufen, much hurt, "but I am "a man of honour."—Every one knows the epigrammatic anfwer of Mr. Michel, when the king afked him, in the war of feven years, Do you imagine that God is your ally alfo? Notwithftanding this, Frederic had as much efteem for Michel as for any man in the world. Michel was often admitted to his table for feveral weeks fucceffively. A little time before the battle gained fo feafonably at Leigniz, the king found himfelf in the greateft danger: before him he had three armies of Ruffians; and every body believed that the horrible tragedy which the half of Europe was engaged in with him, was about to clofe. I was told by Mr. Sulzer and Mr. Cat, who, as his majefty's readers, had free accefs to his tent, that he was already thinking of fpiking up his cannon; and that he begged Michel, in as preffing a manner as Cato begged his friends at Utica, to leave him. Michel,

who

who thought every thing irrecoverably loſt, burnt all his papers ; but he did not quit Frederic.

The following anecdote deſerves to be mentioned here, though it has been printed already. His majeſty being informed that a corporal in his guards, a handſome young fellow, and at the ſame time very brave, wore through vanity a watch chain, to which, for want of a watch, he had affixed a leaden bullet, in order to know the truth of this circumſtance, ſent for him under ſome pretence or other. " Corporal," ſaid the king, " you muſt be brave and economical " both, to have ſaved ſo much of your pay as to " purchaſe a watch."—" I flatter myſelf that I am " brave," replied the corporal ; " but my watch " is worth very little."—Frederic pulling out his watch, which was of gold, ſet with diamonds, ſaid, " My watch points to five ; what o'clock " is it by yours ?" The corporal, with a trembling hand drawing out the leaden bullet from his fob, returned, " Mine, ſire, points neither " to five o'clock nor to ſix o'clock ; but it tells " me plainly what kind of a death I muſt die " for your majeſty." The king was ſo highly pleaſed with this anſwer, that he gave the corporal his own watch ; ſaying, " Here, take this, " in order that you may ſee every day the " hour when you are to die for me."

There

There is no crowned head, undoubtedly, who would not give a watch ſet with brilliants to obtain ſo pleaſing an anſwer; though there are no people in the world who ought to be ſo cautious in their gifts as princes, or more prudent and wiſe in their liberality.

Mankind never perhaps diſplay ſo much folly, impertinence, and avarice, as in their pretenſions, demands, and ſolicitations, when they once know that emperors, queens, or kings are ready to give and to do good. This folly is carried farther in Germany than can well be credited; and of this I had many proofs and examples.

Goodneſs of heart in a ſovereign is, however, the moſt reſpectable of qualities, notwithſtanding the abuſe which may be made of it, and the facility with which people forget it when the royal benefactor approaches the grave. It appears to me that Frederic the Great held it as a maxim, not to ſhew all his goodneſs, for fear that an improper uſe might be made of it. He often concealed within his breaſt a very ſtrong deſire of being uſeful to ſome man of merit, of advancing him in the world, and of rewarding him; but he often did more than the objects of his favour could hope, and that when they leaſt expected it. He knew alſo that a monarch often gains more by fear than

by

by love. He was too well acquainted with the human heart not to know likewiſe, that the great attention and zeal for his ſervice, which he required in all things, were not ſo eaſily obtained by love, which cannot always be depended on from mankind, as by the fear which is univerſally inſpired by the force of authority.

A miniſter who ſerved Frederic a number of years, and with whom he had more than a thouſand conferences, often ſaid, that though the king treated him always politely, and never ſhewed the leaſt diſpleaſure againſt him, yet he thought, every time he was introduced to his majeſty, "To-day, perhaps, I ſhall loſe my em-"ployment, my honour, and my fortune."—The ſevereſt and moſt cutting ſpeech however that Frederic ever made to any miniſter, was the following: "Do you think that I have need of "your eyes to ſee?"

Frederic the Great was a friend, and for many years, to people who perhaps rejoiced at his death.

It ſometimes happens, that to thoſe who follow and obſerve the motions of a monarchical ſtate, there is no epoch more intereſting than that when a riſing ſun is about to take the place of that which is ſetting. The report of the king having enjoyed good reſt during the night,

was

was ſufficient to make a great number of people of the firſt rank at Berlin grow pale; and they trembled leſt the moths ſhould attack their mourning, which had been bought for ſome time. I had occaſion to make ſeveral other obſervations, which diſplaying the like paſſions, and the like ſpirit of intrigue, inſpired me with the utmoſt indignation; and afflicted me the more, as I ſaw the nobleſt conduct purſued, at the ſame time, at Potſdam: and I am firmly perſuaded that an honeſt and rational prince, who wiſhes to render himſelf agreeable to his ſucceſſor, cannot accompliſh his end better than by ſacrificing himſelf, with love and fidelity, for the monarch who is ſtill on the throne. But, in all courts, the minds of the courtiers are, on ſuch occaſions, too much agitated and deranged; the fear of being diſmiſſed, which continually haunts them, renders them often diſſemblers and traitors. It baniſhes from hearts, whoſe good qualities parchment cannot preſerve, integrity, true greatneſs of ſoul, and ſtability in their manner of thinking and acting. The air of a court, which is always a little peſtilential, renders the beſt heads weak, and deſtroys their energy. There greatneſs in thinking and acting, as well as other valuable qualities, diſappear; there warlike valour is changed ed into political effeminacy, and the moſt reſolute firmneſs into ſimple volition; there men become abſolute women; and it is there, in ſhort, that the baſeſt ſcoundrels dare to talk of probity, fidelity, and honour; virtues with which they can never be acquainted, becauſe they are inſenſible to every thing but their own private intereſt, and that of their families.

Such ſouls, deſtitute of energy and vigour, can diſplay nothing but baſeneſs, timidity, and weakneſs; the head of the ſtate is the ſpring of all their actions, and the ſole object of their attention. Even in the pettieſt courts of Germany, in which there is little to be either gained or loſt, a courtier is to-day an atheiſt, and to-morrow believes in Jeſus Chriſt, Lavater, or the Devil: all theſe to him are the ſame, for he never thinks or ſpeaks but as his highneſs. This court ſpirit, of which I am ſpeaking, is however obliged ſometimes to yield to the warlike ſpirit; eſpecially in great courts, where there are always great intereſts to be diſcuſſed. There is a very wide difference between a military veteran of Spartan courage, expert in his profeſſion, poſſeſſed of fidelity, openneſs, and probity; and one of thoſe creeping inſects of a court, deceitful, and abounding in duplicity, and who under a ſpecious outſide conceals

ceals nothing but fraud, ſhame, hypocriſy, weakneſs, and cowardice: But a great, good, faithful, wiſe, and active monarch, who loves his people, and eſteems his army, and who retains only great men around him, will always be a terror to the moſt ſkilful court Proteus, however hackneyed in the ways of deception. Under ſuch a ſovereign, the moſt artful courtier never exerciſes his baſe occupation but with fear; and he can neither be an obſtacle to the advancement of real merit, nor cauſe one uſeful and enlightened man to be diſmiſſed. We ought, however, to be very careful not to judge of a whole nation from the baſe and ignoble ſentiments of a few contemptible individuals. The Brandenburgers and Pruſſians always ſhewed their love and admiration of Frederic the Great, at a time when he diſcharged with pain thoſe duties which the father and defender of a ſtate can never entirely diveſt himſelf of. When the news of Frederic's death were ſpread abroad, every other ſentiment gave place to that of an affliction univerſally felt by his ſubjects; and all ſhared in the general grief. Notwithſtanding the love which the Brandenburgers bore to the new monarch, notwithſtanding their deſire for ſeeing him king, and notwithſtanding the mildneſs and greatneſs of mind with which they beheld Frederic William the Second govern them, and the moderation, wifdom, and fpirit, with which he protected the right of the houfe of Orange, and of his fifter—I cannot help obferving, that the forrow and confternation difplayed during the funeral ceremony of Frederic the Great at Potfdam, prove how difficult it is to forget a truly great man. This monarch, as every great mind when placed on the throne ought to be, was conftantly the fame; that is to fay, always equally good. It was this difpofition towards perfeverance, carried perhaps too far in certain objects, which induced him to preferve his errors. Refpectable divines have often afked me, if the king on his deathbed had not returned to the bofom of the church; if he had never teftified any change, or fhewn any doubt, refpecting his religious fentiments; and if he had perfifted in incredulity to the laft moment of his life. It is with great pain that I find myfelf obliged, in order that I may not betray the interefts of truth, to declare that Frederic never believed in the immortality of the foul; and that even in the hour of death he had no more belief in the chriftian religion than in phyficians and their art.

Frederic allowed the people of Berlin the greateft

greateſt freedom in their opinions; but this freedom was never carried ſo far as to tolerate incredulity. The king wiſhed his ſubjects to think freely; and he conſequently renounced thoſe rights of authority which, in certain objects, ought never to ſhackle a free people. He preached up liberty; and every thing in morals, as well as in religion, degenerated into mental anarchy both at court and in the city. Notwithſtanding this ſituation of affairs, Frederic never ſhewed any inclination for reſtoring order; and the reſult was, that irreligion and deiſm became faſhionable. The king indeed wiſhed for a liberty confined within wiſe and juſt boundaries: but ſome of thoſe men who call themſelves *enlightened* * oppoſed every reſtraint on opinions; and *enlightened* women ſet no bounds to their inclinations and paſſions. Before the eyes even of their wives, and in the open day, the former cauſed proſtitutes to be brought to them, with as little ceremony or myſtery as people obſerve when they ſend for a bottle of wine, or an ounce of tobacco: and the women ſurpaſſed their huſbands in follow-

* People will continue to make uſe of this expreſſion to denote thoſe free-thinkers who at preſent abound in Berlin, and who form a kind of ſect dangerous to reaſon and good morals.

ing

ing their own inclinations ; through the effect, in a great meaſure, of that joy and enthuſiaſm which they experienced on ſeeing *light* diffuſed throughout Berlin.

Several of them, very honeſt women in other reſpects, were unfaithful to their huſbands, becauſe they were deiſts ; that is to ſay, very *enlightened* women. Female infidelity and divorces became as common at Berlin as they were at the moſt corrupted period of the Roman empire. Some of the moſt *enlightened* people of faſhion inſtituted dances in which they danced naked ; and formed expenſive eſtabliſhments, till then unheard of, to facilitate the libertiniſm of old dowagers. The clergymen of Berlin, the ableſt preachers in Europe, were hooted from ſociety, becauſe they ſtill lived in *obſcurity* ; that is to ſay, becauſe they ſtill believed in the religion of Jeſus. Deiſm was preached up in the country pulpits by young miniſters, who repeated there what they had heard when preceptors in great families at Berlin : they laughed at the conſiſtory ; and preached in tied hair, like deiſtical corporals. In this manner the cities were *enlightened* ; and the country ſoon was in the ſame ſituation. But this pretended light made no where ſo much progreſs as at Potſdam. The principles of deiſm, and *this progreſs*

greſs of reaſon, were there carried to ſuch a length, as ſome officers of the king's houſehold informed me, that, during the laſt ten years, above three hundred people had committed ſuicide at Potſdam only.

All theſe diſorders at Potſdam and Berlin are not however to be attributed to the king; for it was impoſſible for him to oppoſe what his ſubjects abſolutely would have, and what he could not alter.

The miniſters of the principality of Neufchatel had a diſpute on the eternity of future puniſhments; and the greater part of them were of opinion that they muſt be eternal. Thoſe who oppoſed this opinion, begged Frederic to puniſh ſuch of their brethren as diſſented from them; but his majeſty replied, "If my "ſubjects of Neufchatel wiſh to be eternally "damned, they may do as they chooſe." Frederic thought, no doubt, in the ſame manner reſpecting the *progreſs of reaſon* at Berlin.

It was neceſſary that a Frederic William ſhould come to ſet bounds to ſuch exceſſes. This prince wrote to preſident Seidlitz, at Breſlau—"As for my part, I am againſt all re-"ſtraint upon conſcience; and I leave every "one to follow his own creed. But I will never "ſuffer the Chriſtian religion to be trampled

"under

"under foot in my dominions. I will never "permit my people to be encouraged to de- "spise the Bible; nor the standard of deism, "infidelity, and materialism to be publicly "erected."—The hereditary prince, son to the present sovereign, an amiable and spirited young man, has openly manifested, at Berlin, that he has adopted judicious and respectable principles of religion.

But, in the time of Frederic the Great, the greatest indifference prevailed respecting this head. It is well known what religious sentiments he entertained. He more than once testified to me, that he adhered, in every thing, to the principles exposed in the *Works of the Philosopher of Sans-Souci*; and I expected that he would not proceed farther: but, after the publication of his works, his religious principles became still worse. Luchesini, however, did every thing that an honest man could do; he brought him back from atheism to deism: and I was very much surprised to find, during my residence at Potsdam, that he spoke much more of the latter than he had done for many years. But he however generally admitted only a few of the received principles of the deists; he then often repeated his ancient opinions, and seemed to be very anxious that people should comprehend him well. Some might therefore conclude that Frederic fluctuated very much in his religious opinions towards the close of his life, and that he was often in doubt whether he should not adopt others. But those who might judge in this manner would undoubtedly be deceived; for I well know that, though his majesty listened attentively to every objection made to him on this head, he remained always firm and unshaken in his sentiments.

I shall here relate, and in a few words, what is known to only a few persons. Frederic the Great never believed, not even at the moment of his death, in the christian religion, or the immortality of the soul; though he was not perhaps always free from uneasiness, in this respect, in the latter part of his life. He shewed a great spirit of toleration towards those who thought differently from him, and who even told him so; and he was mild and indulgent to enthusiasts, fanatics, and fools. Of this he gave a convincing proof, a little while before his death, in his behaviour towards a person who endeavoured to bring him within the pale of the church. Amongst the letters which had arrived one day, and which the king delivered into the hands of his cabinet secretaries, there

was

was one without any ſignature, which ſurpriſed them ſo much that they brought it back to his majeſty. The author, from conſcientious motives, repreſented to the king, out of reſpect and love for him, that, though he had been incredulous all his life-time, there was ſtill room for him to amend, and return to his duty; but that, as he was on the brink of the grave, he had not a moment to loſe, unleſs he wiſhed to go to that place where there are gnaſhing of teeth and eternal wailings, and to be *roaſted in hell* throughout all eternity. The ſame evening the king made a preſent of this letter to Lucheſini; ſaying, "You ſee how careful they "are of my ſoul."

Frederic often joked reſpecting death, when he had the glaſs in his hand. His letters to d'Alembert, at the time when that philoſopher was approaching towards his end, contain ſublime conſolations, replete with the moſt ſtoic philoſophy againſt the dread of ceaſing to exiſt.

Count Lucheſini aſked me however, one day, at Potſdam, in what manner his majeſty's fears reſpecting death might be quieted; as he was not ſuſceptible of that pleaſing conſolation which ariſes to thoſe who believe in the immortality of the ſoul. Comfort him, ſaid I, by repreſenting to him the immortality of his

name;

name; the indelible remembrance of every thing great and ſublime that he has done, and of all the good actions he has performed; and, laſtly, by ſhewing him that all theſe will live a long time after him. The king, as he himſelf has often told me, is not afraid of death, and I believe it; but he hates and deteſts it, and would wiſh to oppoſe it if poſſible. Suffer him to deny, to the laſt, the immortality of the ſoul; for in this point you will never be able to convert him. But tell him boldly, and without ceaſing, that he has done more than any king before him could do in a ſimilar ſituation; and that all he has done has taken too deep root not to expand and flouriſh till the remoteſt period of futurity. Repeat to him, and even proclaim with a loud voice, in his lateſt moments, that *the Pruſſian Eagle ſhall never be humbled.*

Tender and ſublime ſoul! thou wonder of the eighteenth century! at once philoſopher, hero, legiſlator, and conqueror—monarch whoſe name ſhall live to the end of ages, and from whoſe glory every thing has already been ſeparated that jealouſy or malevolence could throw upon it with a view to tarniſh it—thy earthly frame, depoſited at Potſdam, is not the only part which remains of thee. Placed in the abode of the immortals, thou art now near thy Marcus

Aurelius; and this production is only the smallest of the flowers scattered over thy tomb. Thy name will be always engraven on my heart, as the soft and tender sound of thy last words—*Zimmermann, remember the good old man that you have seen here!*

FINIS.

A
SHORT ADDRESS
TO THE
PUBLIC,
ON THE
PRACTICE OF CASHIERING MILITARY OFFICERS WITHOUT A TRIAL;
AND A
VINDICATION
OF THE
CONDUCT AND POLITICAL OPINIONS OF THE AUTHOR.
TO WHICH IS PREFIXED,
HIS CORRESPONDENCE
WITH THE
SECRETARY AT WAR.
By HUGH LORD SEMPILL.

LONDON:
PRINTED FOR J. JOHNSON, No. 72, ST. PAUL'S CHURCH-YARD.

M,DCC,XCIII.

[Price ONE SHILLING.]

CORRESPONDENCE

WITH THE

SECRETARY AT WAR,

AND OTHER

OFFICIAL PAPERS.

War Office, Nov. 30, 1792.

MY LORD,

I HAVE it in command from the King, to notify to your Lordſhip, that his Majeſty has no further occaſion for your ſervices; and that you are, from this day, no longer to conſider yourſelf as a Lieutenant in the Third Regiment of Foot Guards: But his Majeſty has been graciouſly pleaſed to permit you to receive from the officer, whom his Majeſty ſhall think fit to appoint, to the vacant Lieutenancy, the regulated value of that Commiſſion.

I am,
My Lord,
Your Lordſhip's
Moſt obedient Servant,
GEO. YONGE.

Right Hon.
Lord Sempill.

St. James's Hotel,
30th Nov. 1792.

SIR,

I HAVE juſt received your letter, informing me that you have it in command from the King to notify to me, that his Majeſty has no further occaſion for my ſervices; and that I am, from this day, no longer to conſider myſelf as a Lieutenant in the third regiment of Guards: but you do not aſſign any reaſon for a meaſure ſo unuſal as ſuperſeding an officer, whoſe conduct has not been impeached.

As I am not ſenſible of having acted, in any reſpect, inconſiſtent with my duty, or that any part of my conduct through life has been deſerving of the King's diſpleaſure, I have to requeſt that you will, in juſtice to a character, hitherto, I truſt, unreproached, inform me of the reaſons which have moved you, or the King's miniſters, to adviſe his Majeſty to diſpoſe of my commiſſion in a manner ſo injurious, which I ſo little expected, and as little deſerve.

If I have been accuſed of having done any thing which would, in the opinion of his Majeſty's miniſters, diſqualify me for my ſituation, I cannot doubt that you will give me an opportunity fairly to meet the charge, and to prove, as I hope I ſhall at all times be able to do, that my conduct has been conſiſtent

 with

with my duty as an Officer and a Citizen.

I have the honor to be,

Sir,

Your, &c.

SEMPILL.

To Sir George Yonge.

St. James's Hotel,
30th Nov. 1792.

To Col. Grinfield.

SIR,

I HAVE received a letter from the Secretary at War, telling me that he has it in command from the King to notify to me, that I am no longer to consider myself as a Lieutenant in the third regiment of Guards, but without informing me of the reason of my removal. And as a measure so unusual, may be thought to reflect on my character, I have to request, that you will give me the satisfaction to inform me, whether my conduct as an officer, has, at any time, ſince I have been under your command, been deſerving of cenſure.

I have the honor to be, &c.

SEMPILL.

Orderly Room, 3d. Gds.
Dec. 1, 1792.

MY LORD,

I HAVE the honor to acknowledge the receipt of your Lordſhip's letter of this date; in anſwer thereto I moſt readily acknowledge, that ſince the regiment has been under my command, I have every reaſon to be ſatisfied with your military conduct.

I have the honor to be,
My Lord,
Your Lordſhip's
Moſt obedient and
Humble Servant,
W. GRINFIELD.
1ſt Maj[r]. Comm[g]. 3d Gs.

Lord Sempill.

3d Guards, Orderly Room,
Dec. 1, 1792.

My Lord,

I AM directed by the commanding officer to acquaint your Lordſhip, that he received, yeſterday, his Majeſty's order, through the Secretary at War, of which the encloſed is a copy.—In compliance therewith, I am to ſignify to your Lordſhip that the regulated price (1500l.) of the commiſſion lately held by you, is at your command, in the hands of Meſſrs. Roſs and Ogilvie, agents to the regiment.

I am your Lordſhip's
Very humble ſervant,
JOHN HENRY LOFT.
Enſign and Acting Adjutant.

Lord Sempill.

War Office, Nov. 30, 1792.

SIR,

HAVING this day, by his Majeſty's order, notified to Lord Sempill, that his Majeſty has no further occaſion for his ſervices, and that he is no longer to conſider himſelf as a Lieutenant in the third regiment of Foot Guards, but that his Majeſty allows Lord Sempill to receive from the officer whom his Majeſty ſhall think fit to appoint to the vacant Lieutenancy, the regulated value of that commiſſion: I have the honor to acquaint you therewith for the information of the Duke of Argyle, and to deſire that his Grace's recommendation of the officers for purchaſe in conſequence of the ſaid vacancy, may

may be tranſmitted to me with as little delay as poſſible.

I have the honor to be,

Sir,

Your moſt obedient

Humble ſervant,

(Signed) GEO. YONGE.

Officer commanding the 3d regt. of Foot Guards.

War Office, Dec. 3d, 1792.

My Lord,

I AM to acknowledge the receipt of your Lordſhip's letter of the 30th of laſt month.

When I informed your Lordſhip, that his Majeſty had no further occaſion for your ſervice, and that you would be allowed to receive the regulated value of your late commiſſion in the 3d regiment of Foot Guards, I communicated

communicated all that I had in command from his Majesty to notify to your Lordship.

I have the honor to be,
My Lord,
Your Lordship's
Most obedient
Humble servant,
GEO. YONGE.

Right Hon.
Lord Sempill.

St. James Hotel,
Dec. 14, 1792.

SIR,

I requested in my letter to you of the 30th November, that you would inform me of the reasons of my being superseded, and that you would give me an opportunity of vindicating my character; to which you gave me no other answer, than that you communicated to me all that you had in command

command from his Majeſty. I have now to requeſt, before I appeal to another tribunal, that I may be tried by a court martial, which I conceive I have a right to demand.

I have likewiſe to inform you, that I received, in conſequence of your directions to the commanding officer, a notification, that the regulated value of my commiſſion was lodged at the agent's, which I have declined accepting, until I inform myſelf whether my receiving it would bar my claim to promotion.

I have the honour to be, &c.

SEMPILL.

To the Secretary at War.

War Office,
Dec. 20, 1792.

MY LORD,

I AM honored with your Lordſhip's letter of the 14th inſt. and having

having yesterday laid it before his Majesty, I am commanded to acquaint you that his Majesty has not thought fit to grant the request contained in that letter.

Your Lordship, not being at present possessed of any rank in the army, can have no claim to promotion—and of course, your future situation in that respect, will, in no degree, be affected by your acceptance or by your refusal of the sum which his Majesty has been graciously pleased to allow you to receive, as the regulated value of your late commission in the Foot Guards.

I have the honor to be,
Your Lordship's
Most obedient humble servant,
GEO. YONGE.

Lord Sempill.

MY correſpondence with the Secretary at War being now cloſed, I take the liberty to appeal (though ſuch appeals be proſcribed by the new Burkean code,*) from the fiat of the court, to the juſtice of the nation.

In May or June laſt, having been informed by the Adjutant that I was eldeſt Lieutenant, and officially required to declare if I would purchaſe, I anſwered, that I would purchaſe at the regulated price; and a few days after, in a letter to the Commanding Officer or Adjutant, I propoſed to give four thouſand pounds for the Captain-Lieutenancy,†

* See Mr. Burke's ſpeech on Le Brun's Report, in the Morning Chronicle of Dec. 29.

† The regulated value of a company is the ſame with that of a Lieutenant-Coloneley of the line, 3,500l.; that of a Captain-Lieutenancy 2,600l.

provided

provided I ſhould not be required to give a certificate reſpecting the regulation; which propoſal was rejected. I afterwards relinquiſhed my claim as eldeſt, in favour of Captain Barnet, who was recommended in the uſual form: but the Secretary at War inſiſted on Colonel Pelham, the Captain-Lieutenant, ſelling to the Marquis of Huntley. I relinquiſhed a ſecond time my claim as firſt for purchaſe in favour of Captain Barnet, who was promoted to a company: and though Lord Huntley was appointed ſome weeks before Colonel Barnet, the King, with his Majeſty's wonted love of juſtice, marked as ſtrongly as poſſible his diſapprobation of the conduct of the Secretary at War, by ordering Mr. Barnet's commiſſion to bear the ſame date with Lord Huntley's, which, according to the rules of the army, made Mr. Barnet, who was an old captain, precede Lord Huntley.

I have

I have mentioned theſe circumſtances, in order to eſtabliſh my claim to rank above Captain Stuart, who, by my removal, became eldeſt Lieutenant; in caſe my ſervices ſhould at any future time be accepted of.

A

SHORT ADDRESS, &c.

THE Secretary at War having denied my requeſt of a trial, and refuſed to inform me of the reaſons of my being ſuperceded, the vindication of my character, as well as my duty to the public, to which every officer, civil and military, is accountable, obliges me to make this appeal.

I ſolemnly declare, and thoſe who know my habitual indolence, as well as my marked abhorrence of faction, will readily believe, that I am not influenced either by private intereſt or party ſpirit. I have not even communicated my intention to write this vindication to any perſon, except a learned friend, for whoſe opinion I have the higheſt reſpect, whom I had occaſion to ſee a few days ago on private buſineſs, and who gave me his advice in theſe words: "Publiſh a vindication of your conduct "as an officer, and a declaration of "your political principles."

No particular part of my conduct is denounced, though the whole of it is attacked by inſinuation. But the refuſal of a court-martial, the commanding officer's letter declaring my military conduct to be blameleſs, as well as the teſtimony of the corps, ſufficiently warrant me to aſſert, that my conduct, as an officer, in the moſt extenſive ſenſe

of

of the phraſe, is unimpeached, and irreproachable.

It muſt, then, be my political conduct which has incurred ſo ſtrong a mark of the King's diſpleaſure, or rather of the diſpleaſure of his Majeſty's Miniſters.

And it is of no ſmall importance to the army, and to the public, to conſider, whether an influence, unconſtitutional and dangerous, is not derived from the power of caſhiering officers, without a trial: Whether it does not prevent men of independent principles from ſerving in the army, and enſlave thoſe who have laid out too great a proportion of their fortunes in purchaſing commiſſions, without having been aware that they were ſurrendering the freedom of opinion, and relinquiſhing the franchiſes of citizens.

It was not in the ſtrong features of patriotiſm, ſo elegantly delineated by the Roman and Grecian hiſtorians, that I was taught to trace the character of a freeman; nor in the antiquities of Greece and Rome, that I was taught to ſtudy the principles of conſtitutional liberty; but in the political conſtitutions of the Anglo-Saxons, the wiſeſt, and the moſt friendly to mankind, which hiſtory has furniſhed for the inſtruction of men.

I was taught, from the firſt moment that I was capable of knowing what right and duty mean, that it is the chief right, and the chief duty of every Briton, to claim that conſtitutional freedom, which the wiſdom and virtue of our Saxon anceſtors aſſerted and eſtabliſhed, and to reſiſt every attempt to leſſen or to deſtroy it, whether by the towering pretenſions of prerogative, or by the inſidious and more dangerous attacks of ſecret influence.

Alfred, who brought the Saxon conſtitution as near perfection as the barbarity and ſuperſtition of the age would admit of, is the only legiſlator, the late National Aſſembly of France not excepted, who knew how to govern the people by the people, to unite the parts, and to organize the whole, by the principle of repreſentation, the ignorance of which principle prevented the perfection of the ancient republics. And it is impoſſible to contemplate this monument of wiſdom and patriotiſm, without regretting, that an opportunity was loſt, on the expulſion of the tyrannical race of Stuart, when the only two blots in the Saxon government, the villanage of the peaſants, and the influence of the clergy, were both nearly wiped away, to regain theſe bleſſings, our long loſt rights, and to perfect a a conſtitution the admiration of every ſucceeding age; the only one which has ever furniſhed the means of collecting the public will, and of a conſtant exerciſe of political liberty; the loſs of which, by the Norman conqueſt, cauſed ſo much blood to be ſhed during ſix centuries, and the reſtoration of which would probably prevent a drop being ſhed, for ſix centuries to come.

With theſe impreſſions, I have beheld the ſtruggles of contending parties, without enliſting under the banners of either.

When

When I was called upon to exercise the function of an elective peer, I did it in the manner which I conceived to be most conducive, not to the interest of those with whom I acted only, but to that of the country. I confess that I at first declined voting, because I thought that the peerage elections had long been a disgrace to the peerage and to the nation. When a party was formed professedly to support the independence of the peerage, and to resist ministerial interference, I heartily joined it, to shew my abhorrence of venality, and my contempt of the insolent and illegal mandates of a Secretary of State.

If these sentiments, and this conduct are deserving of the king's displeafure, I confefs that I have deferved it.

In order to vindicate my conduct in Scotland, it is neceffary that I fhould curforily review (I will endeavour to do it in very few words) the events and the polity of former times, which had reduced the country to the deplorable fituation that called forth the exertions of the excellent citizens with whom I acted, whofe rights it is my duty, and fhall be the bufinefs of my life, to defend.

The union of the crowns, and the removal of the feat of government, enabled the King to alienate the affections of the Scotch nobility from their country, and, by corrupting the Parliament,

Parliament, to enſlave the people, among whom he had, a ſhort time before, been the moſt limited monarch in Europe. The Scotch, who had uniformly, till then, reſiſted every ſtretch of the prerogative, with a firmneſs ſcarcely to be equalled in hiſtory, were, by the influence of the Engliſh treaſury, completely ſubdued.

From the union of the crowns, till the union of the kingdoms, Scotland was treated like a conquered province. Such acts of parliament as were contrary to the new notions of prerogative, were mutilated or deſtroyed; and every attempt to aſſert her ancient rights, or the freedom of trade, was conſidered as an act of rebellion.

The union of the kingdoms, garbled as the treaty was, rendered her ſituation ſomewhat more tolerable. But the improvement, owing to the defect of the repreſentation, and the confirmation of the feudal juriſdiction was ſo ſlow, as to be ſcarcely perceptible in fifty years. After the paſſing of the juriſdiction act, the progreſs was comparatively rapid. In one town, the enterprizing ſpirit of a few individuals, in ſpite of every obſtacle, was attended with wonderful ſucceſs. Glaſgow, in 1770, enjoyed a very great proportion of the American colony trade; and ſome of her merchants had acquired very conſiderable fortunes. But the benefit of this trade was felt in the neighbourhood of Glaſgow only; and even there it was not of ſo much ſer-

vice

vice as the manufactures of Paisley; for the greatest part of the return, instead of increasing domestic industry, was employed in purchasing the manufactured commodities of other countries to export to America.

The independence of America gave a sudden and a very beneficial turn to the trade of Scotland.

When Dr. Smith published his book, which shews that "*Colonies are commercially useless, as well as politically mischievous*," those who thought themselves interested in the continuance of the monopoly, and who could not controvert the justness of his reasoning, were rash enough to assert, that experience evinced the fallacy of his theory; but the American Revolution, and the consequent Revolution in the trade of Scotland,

Scotland, are a practical proof of its truth.

The capital which had been forced, by the monopoly, into the colony trade, returned to its natural channel, and is now employed in manufactures at home, particularly in the manufacture of muslin, and a variety of cotton goods, and puts in motion, in this new employment, at least ten times as much domestic industry as the colony trade, which was said to be so advantageous.

The American Revolution is still more important in a political, than in a commercial point of view. It exhibits a model of a well organized community, of a government of all by all, which affords protection alike to every citizen, without distinction of religion, or of rank; and forms a striking contrast with

with the European governments, where there is one law for the rich, and another for the poor.

The American pays no more to the expence of the government, than he is ſenſible is neceſſary, and he ſees expended; and not, as in ſome European governments, where the induſtrious labourer is robbed, by taxes, of one half of the earnings of his labour, to fatten the profligate tools of power, and to pamper the inſolence of thoſe, who, confounding truſt with right, claim to be tyrants, by the title of inheritance, or of eloquence, and to revel on the plunder of the ſwiniſh multitude.*

The

* In every country where the government is, in any degree, ariſtocratic, the rich and the privileged have invented a variety of epithets, to denote their own excellence, and the inferiority of their fellow citizens, who have no property in the land, and who ſupport themſelves by labour, or trade.

In

The people of Scotland are bound by laws which they have no voice in making, and are forced to pay taxes, to which they have not consented by themselves or their representatives. The burgesses are divested of all the franchises of citizens, and, as if they were

In France, before the late Revolution, so justly execrated by those who are sensible of the blessing of a wise dispensation of privileges, places, and pensions, all those who did not inherit privilege, hold offices under the crown, or who had not amassed, from the plunder of the public, by farms and contracts, fortunes sufficient to purchase distinction, were distinguished by the appellations of *peuple* and *bas peuple*.

In the classic language of an English statesman, so celebrated for his humanity, and his learning, that he has been called the ornament of the British parliament, and of British literature, the *peuple*, *bas peuple* of Britain, namely, nine in a hundred of the whole community, are distinguished by the elegant, and emphatic epithet, of the swinish multitude; an epithet expressive of their having lately disturbed the festive board of their lords, and offended the delicate ears of the courtiers, by angry notes, and inharmonious accents, by grunting out complaints of the coldness of their sties, and scantiness of their food.

less

lefs entitled to protection, than the other disfranchifed citizens of Britain, they are fubject to fine, imprifonment, and corporal punifhment, at the difcretion of their magiftrates, who have long been fuffered, with impunity, to alienate the common property of the boroughs, for their private emolument, to levy taxes, of their own authority, and to enforce their arbitrary exactions, by quartering foldiers, a refinement on the ufe of a ftanding army, fo much the more dangerous, that it can be practifed without bloodfhed.

The fpirit of the people of Scotland had long been broken by oppreffion; to their ancient grievances was added, the feverity of the excife laws, which crufhed their feeble efforts, and nipped induſtry in the bud. The additional taxes on the neceſſaries of life made it impoſſible, until the late improvements in machinery, to carry manufactured commodities to a foreign market.

The manufacturers of Scotland have likewiſe ſuffered, in common with the Engliſh, from the deſtructive power which an imperfect and corrupt repreſentation gives to the miniſter, to grant a monopoly to the rich manufacturer, by increaſing the taxes on certain articles, and cruſhing the manufacturer of ſmall capital. Such abuſes are not to be feared from a patriotic miniſter, and a virtuous parliament, like the preſent; but a corrupt parliament, and an intriguing miniſter, might, by ſuch practices, totally annihilate commerce and liberty.

A comparifon of the American government with the boafted conftitution of Britain, naturally led the people of Scotland in general, and the burgeffes in particular, to difcufs political queftions, and to confider of a remedy for the intolerable abufes, to which they were afhamed of having fo long fubmitted. They brought a bill into Parliament for a reform in the internal government of the boroughs, to make the magiftrates accountable in a court of juftice, for their adminiftration of the public funds; for redrefs againft arbitrary exactions; and to put a ftop to the practice of felf-election, the foundation of a fyftem of corruption and tyranny, unequalled in the hiftory of abufes.

I was called upon to affift the burgeffes in their laudable attempt; and after their petitions had been for ſeveral years treated with inſolent contempt by the Miniſter, and neglected by the Houſe of Commons, I was aſtoniſhed to hear it propoſed, in the Convention of Delegates, that they ſhould not apply for a Parliamentary Reform, but only for a reform in the internal government of the boroughs. I declared it to be my opinion, that they could not expect redreſs without a reform in the repreſentation, which, in England, is but a mockery, and in Scotland, does not bear even the ſemblance of a real repreſentation.

If theſe ſentiments, and this conduct, are deſerving of the King's diſpleaſure, I confeſs that I heartily deſerve it.

While

While the people of Europe were contemplating, with aſtoniſhment, the ſucceſs of America, her peace, happineſs, and incredibly rapid increaſe of wealth, which immediately followed ten years of civil war:—While the diſfranchiſed citizens of Britain were looking, with admiration and envy, at a government ſupported at ſo little expence, which gives every encouragement to induſtry, and ſecures an equality of rights to all its members; the abettors of deſpotiſm, thoſe intereſted in the continuation of abuſes, were employing their venal pens to deride the American government, to perſuade the people that ſuch a government is fit for a poor and an infant ſtate only; that any reaſoning on the practice of it in America cannot be applied to the European States, where the manners of the people have been long formed, and their characters fixed, and where the governments are moulded to the manners and character of the people; as if the minds of a whole nation could be so debilitated by the vices of its government, and so depraved by habit, as to prefer a government by the sword to a government by reason, and arbitrary power to equal aws; as if men could be rendered, by long oppression, incapable of the exercise of freedom, and insensible of the blessings of liberty, a desire of which is common to every race of men, in every age, in every clime, and in every possible variety of situation; a desire, planted by the hand of nature, and which cannot be extirpated by the ingenuity of man.

While the nations of Europe were looking to America for instruction, and,

and, in ſpite of all the exertions of proſtituted abilities to bewilder their judgment, were convinced of the ſuperiority of her government to their own, one of them reſolved to follow her example, to exerciſe the right, which every people derive from nature, to frame a government for themſelves. And the attention of the reſt of the world is arreſted by a brilliant experiment, to prove the general practicability of a repreſentative government.

All the former revolutions in Europe were only the ſtruggles of contending factions: the moſt beneficial of them did little more than eſtabliſh an ariſtocracy, I confeſs a mild one, on the ruins of the prerogative. That revolution ſettled a government comparatively mild, and improved what is called, perhaps improperly, civil liberty;

but, (leaving delegated power without controul,) afforded no ſecurity that it ſhould not be invaded; and the alterations in the conſtitution of Parliament, ſince that time, have reduced political liberty to an empty name.

Former revolutions had done no more then determine which of the privileged orders ſhould govern the community, and divide the plunder. The principle of the French revolution was to organize the community itſelf: though I do not contend that the work of the conſtituent aſſembly was conſiſtent with the principles on which they pretended to found it.

Aſſociations were formed in this country, at the end of the American war, after the nation had been long torn by faction, and exhauſted by peculation, for the purpoſe of reforming the reprefentation: and though their refolutions were garbled, and their views mifdirected by party cabal, and the intrigues of thofe interefted in the perpetuation of abufes, they fufficiently manifefted the fenfe of the nation; and bound, if any pledge can bind, the principal candidates for popular favour, by public declarations of their political principles, and particularly of their opinions refpecting reprefentation. And the French conftitution was no fooner publifhed in this country, than it was believed, that fuch an example would induce the people to perfect the work, in which, they had lately failed; that Britons, who had fo long boafted of being free, would not fubmit to a fophifticated government, when the French had founded theirs on the principle, that all men are born free and equal.

The man who is bound by a law to which he has not consented, is a slave; and I call our government sophisticated, because, while the legislature is elected by a few, it is pretended that all are virtually represented. The disfranchising statute of the time of Hen. VI. confirmed the government introduced by the conqueror; the Septennial Act was as glaring a violation of the constitution established in 1688.

I have ever been of opinion, that unless these innovations be corrected, and the people restored to their elective rights, the constitution itself must be lost; and I have, therefore, on all occasions, declared myself to be a firm friend to reform—equal representation, and annual parliaments.

I confeſs, and I truſt, that I need not bluſh, when I confeſs, that in my correſpondence with all the ſocieties to which I belong, I have avowed it to be my moſt earneſt wiſh, that the French Revolution might produce a revolution in all the deſpotic governments of Europe, and a regeneration of our own.

We have a ſyſtem of juriſprudence excellent, in many reſpects, but ſo clogged with the remains of feudal barbarity, blended with modern fiction, as to be in many caſes inapplicable, and frequently inexplicable, and to create greater uncertainty than if no law exiſted; and which has been ſo confounded by the ſophiſtry of intriguing judges, that nothing but the ſtern virtue, perhaps, of the preſent bench, could prevent it from becoming a fit engine of despotism. By the tricks of practisioners, and the extortion of the officers of the courts, though reprobated by the judges, who have but a small share of the fees, justice, if it may be so called, is become so expensive, as to make the poor, in many cases even the rich, silently submit to injustice.

We have a hierarchy useless, expensive, and disgraceful. The tythes are a constant source of contention, a constant bar to improvement. The laws against Dissenters would disgrace the code of the most barbarous nation in the universe. I am not the advocate of Secretaries, but of liberty. I should be sorry to see the present establishment give way to Presbyterianism, or to any other form of church discipline: but I would have the word Toleration expunged

punged from our Dictionary, as disgracing the language of a nation that pretends to be free.

I did not hesitate to express my satisfaction at the French Revolution, because it was impossible to behold the struggles of reviving Liberty, without rejoicing at their success; because, I conceive, that no man endowed with the feelings of humanity, can see a nation, subjected to the capricious cruelty of a few, without wishing that they may break their chains on the heads of their oppressors; [illegible] I saw no reason to withhol[illegible]ht tribute of my grat[illegible]eous Patriots, who [illegible], [illegible] Liberty and Happiness, twenty millions of my fellow-low-creatures. I ſaw no reaſon to be aſhamed, or afraid, to join in the general applauſe of a Revolution, which broke the chains of ſuperſtition and prieſt-craft, by diſperſing an army of robbers, and fiends, who had been allowed, for ſo many ages, to prey on the weakneſs of their fellow-men; and while they called themſelves the miniſters of charity and peace, to ſupport themſelves in luxury by extortion and fraud, and to acquire power and emolument, by ſtirring up, in the true ſpirit of the devil, nation againſt nation, and man againſt man.

If theſe be the ſentiments of a Leveller, and an Atheiſt, I am deſerving of both theſe epithets.

If

If I am to give an account of my opinions, as well as of my conduct, and I am asked, What kind of government I think the beſt, I anſwer, that, as far as my ſhallow acquirements enable me to judge, a Repreſentative Government is the beſt. If I am aſked, Whether I think it neceſſary or prudent to give Britain a new Conſtitution, I anſwer, without heſitation, let us perfect the Saxon conſtitution, and we ſhall have little reaſon to envy the French, ſhould the conſtitution, they are about to eſtabliſh, be ever ſo perfect.

As a Briton I wiſh to ſee our government immediately reformed; becauſe I am perſuaded, that without an immediate and a thorough repair, the antient fabric muſt ſoon fall; becauſe I would avert from us, and from our children, the temporary evils which muſt attend

a violent

a violent Revolution, and even the ſmaller inconveniencies, which muſt attend the ſubverſion of antient forms. But no influence ſhall ever make me deny the great truth, that every people derive a right from nature, to alter their government when their ſafety requires it.

As a citizen of the world, I wiſh to ſee the French Republic confirmed, and the Britiſh Conſtitution perfected, as an experiment for the inſtruction of the world, which of the two is the beſt.

If this conduct, and theſe ſentiments, are deſerving of the King's diſpleaſure, I confeſs that I deſerve it: and I am at a loſs to gueſs, by what ſort of conduct, or profeſſions, I may hope for ſo great a ſatisfaction, as His Majeſty's good opinion.

I hope that the King will ſoon have Councellors wiſe enough to know, and honeſt

honeſt enough to tell him, that the real friends of Reform cannot be the enemies of order and peace. I ſhall then beg leave to approach His Majeſty, and to tell him, that I am not the enemy of peace and order, but that I am the avowed and determined enemy of thoſe vices, of which His Majeſty has ever been the enemy, unbounded ambition, tyranny, and peculation.

But I ſhould be unworthy of the good opinion of my country, I ſhould be unworthy of the title of freeman, once the pride of Britons, if I were capable of being deterred from my duty, by the diſpleaſure of a Prince, or the reſentment of a Miniſter.

F I N I S.

CONSIDERATIONS

ON

TWO PAPERS,

PUBLISHED AT

ANTWERP,

RESPECTING

A LOAN FOR 3,600,000 GUILDERS;

TO BE SUBSCRIBED AT THE HOUSES OF

MESSIEURS J. E. WERBROUCK

AND

C. J. M. DE WOLF,

OF THAT CITY.

THE SECOND EDITION.

LONDON:

PRINTED FOR JOHN STOCKDALE, OPPOSITE BURLINGTON HOUSE, PICCADILLY.

1791.

[PRICE TWO SHILLINGS AND SIXPENCE.]

CONSIDERATIONS

ON

TWO PAPERS

PUBLISHED AT

ANTWERP.

BERIGT

Van eene Negotiatie groot *f.* 3,600,000 wiſſel geld voor, Rekeninge van HUNNE KONINGLYKE HOOGHEDEN DEN PRINS VAN WALLES, DEN HERTOG VAN YORK, ende DEN HESTOG VAN CLARENCE, waer van *f.* 1,800,000 wiſſel-geld ten Comptoire van JEAN E. WERBROUCK binnen Antwerpen, ingevolge de Acten en Beſcheeden ter inſpectie der Geld-ſchieters.

I.

DEZE Negotiatie geschied voor eenen termyn van 25 Jaeren, dog na verloop van 15 Jaeren zal'er Jaerlyks een thiende ter respectieve Comptoiren by loting worden afgelost, en de trekking daer van geschieden voor Notaris en getuygen, dus dat het heel Capitael in 25 Jaeren zal gequeten zyn.

II.

De Obligatien zullen zyn van *f.* 1000 wissel-geld ieder; ende door eenen Notaris der Stad Antwerpen tegengeteekend.

III.

Tot verzekeringe van deze Negotiatie verbinden HUNNE KONINGLYKE HOOGHEDEN alle hunne Appanagien, ende de Inkomsten van het Hertogdom van CORNWALLIS, ende van het Bisdom van OSNABURGH, beloopende jaerlyks te saemen ten

 minsten

minsten tot *f.* 1,220,000 wissel-geld, ende bewyzen de zelve generaelyk in *Depositum* in handen van zes Engelsche Heeren van d'eerste distinctie en vermogen, te weten: *den Hertog van Portland, den Hertog van Northumberland, den Graeve Fitzwilliam, de Lords Southampton, Rawdon* ende *Malmsbury*, gezaementlyk met de agtbaere *Thomas Erskine* ende *Arthur Piggot* Ridders, waer van de voornoemde Heeren zig verbinden niet te zullen onthandigen, dan ten voordeele der Geld-schieters.

IV.

Verders zullen'er tot meerder verzekeringe nog jaerlyks dry duyzende Ponden Sterlings uyt hunne Revenuen of Appanagien worden aengeleyd in de geconsolideerde Engelsche Bank Annuiteyten, zoo als de Intresten daer van voortskomende op de gezamentlyke Naemen van dry bekende

Per-

Perſoonen by d'Actens vermeld, om alzoo te dienen tot eenen koelenden Fond voor deze Negociatie.

V.

Den Intreſt, ingaende met 1 Feb. 1791, zal zyn à rato van 5 per Cent 's Jaers betaelbaer in Coupons van zes tot zes maenden ten voorſ. Comptoire; ende aengezien alle de voornoemde Inkomſten ende Appanagien maer en zyn voor den levenstyd van Hunne gemelde KONINGLYKE HOOGHEDEN, ſtaen zy toe, boven den voorſchreven Intreſt, eene Premie van een per Cent 's Jaers voor de gene die het leven van Hunne voorſ. KONINGLYKE HOOGHEDEN zelfs willen verzekeren.

VI.

De gene, die zig zullen vergenoegen met den Intereſt van 5 per Cent, zullen de gemelde

melde levens geassureerd hebben door Persoonen van de eerste distinctie en vermogen, te weten: *den Hertog van Portland, den Graeve Fitzwilliam, den Borg-graeve Malmsbury, Lord Robert Spencer*, ende *Sir Thomas Dundas*, blykens het Project van *Polus* ten voormelde Comptoire te zien.

TRANSLATION.

Notice of a Loan for 3,600,000 gilders, Exchange money, for account of their Royal Highnesses the Prince of Wales, the Duke of York, and the Duke of Clarence, of which 1,800,000 guilders, Exchange money, is to be negociated at the counting house of Jean E. Werbrouck, in Antwerp, agreeable to the deeds and documents for the inspection of the money-lenders.

THIS

I.

THIS Loan is made for a term of 25 years; but after the expiration of 15 years, one-tenth part thereof to be reimburſed at the reſpective offices by way of a Lottery, to be drawn in the preſence of a Notary Publick and witneſſes, ſo that the whole capital ſhall be paid off in 25 years.

II.

The obligations or bonds ſhall be of 1000 guilders Exchange money each, and contra-ſigned by a Notary Publick of the city of Antwerp.

III.

For the ſecurity of this Loan their Royal Highneſſes pledge all their appanages and the revenues of the Dutchy of Cornwall, and of the Biſhoprick of Oſnaburgh, amounting annually together, at leaſt to the ſum of

1,220,000 guilders, Exchange money, and make the ſame over in *depoſitum* (in truſt) in the hands of ſix Engliſh gentlemen of the firſt rank and fortune; viz. The Duke of Portland, the Duke of Northumberland; Earl Fitzwilliam; Lords Southampton, Rawdon, and Malmſbury, jointly with the Hon. Thomas Erſkine and Arthur Pigot, Eſquires; of which the before-mentioned gentlemen bind themſelves not to part with, otherwiſe than for the benefit of the money-lenders.

IV.

Farther, as an additional ſecurity, there ſhall be yearly laid out three thouſand pounds ſterling, out of their revenues or appenages, in the conſolidated Engliſh Bank Annuities, together with the intereſt ariſing therefrom, on the names of three well known perſons mentioned by the deeds, to ſerve as a ſinking fund for this Loan.

V.

The intereſt to commence the firſt of February, 1791, at the rate of 5 *per cent. per ann.* payable on *coupons* (warrants) from ſix to ſix months, at the office before-mentioned: and in conſideration that all the above-mentioned revenues and appenages are only during the lives of their Royal Highneſſes above-named, they grant an annual premium of 1 *per cent.* over and above the ſaid intereſt, to thoſe who chuſe to inſure themſelves, the lives of their ſaid Royal Highneſſes.

VI.

Thoſe who ſhall content themſelves with the intereſt of 5 *per cent.* ſhall have the before-mentioned lives inſured by perſons

of

of the first rank and fortune, viz. the Duke of Portland, the Earl Fitz-William, Viscount Malmsbury, Lord Robert Spencer, and Sir Thomas Dundas, conformable to the form of a policy, to be seen at the office above-mentioned.

RELEVÉ.

Des pieces & actes relatifs a l'emprunt de f. 3,600,000 argent de change, pour compte de leurs Altesses Royales le Prince de GALLES, le Duc de YORK, & le Duc de CLARENCE, dont f. 1,800,000 au bureau de Monsieur Jean E. WERBROUCK à Anvers.

I.

Un acte d'autorisation, signé par leurs Altesses Royales, & témoins en date du 16 Novembre, 1790, par lequelle elles autorisent

risent Mr. Jean E. Werbrouck, & Mr. C. J. M. de Wolf, banquiers à Anvers, d'y ouvrir pour leur compte commun, un emprunt de f. 3,600,000 de change, aux conditions dont on a donné le détail par un prospectus imprimé à cet effet, avec promesse d'assigner en dépôt leurs appanages & revenus entre les mains de six Seigneurs Anglois de la premiere distinction, & de la plus grande fortune, savoir: le Duc de Portland, le Duc de Northumberland, le Comte Fitzwilliam, les Lords Southampton, Rawdon, & Malmsbury, ce que les-dets Seigneurs acceptent par acte au pied de ladite autorisation, & s'engagent d'employer les fonds qui leur parviendront en vertu de l'acte de dépôt conformément aux fins, auxquelles ils sont destinés, savoir, 1° au payement des intérêts annuels de six en six mois, 2° au payement des primes ou assurances sur le pied stipulé, 3° à la retenue annuelle

annuelle de 3000l. ſterling, pour être employées dans les annuités conſolidées de la banque d'Angleterre ſous les noms conjoints de ſa Grandeur le Duc de Portland, de M. Jean E. Werbrouck, & de M. Joſiah Jowett, pour ſervir de fond d'amortiſſement, 4° à la retenue des ſommes qui manqueront pour le rembourſement du capital aux époques préſcrites.

II.

Deux obligations ſolidaires de leurs Alteſſes Royales de f. 1,800,000 de change chacune, l'une en favour de Mr. Jean E. Werbrouck, & l'autre en favour de Mr. C. J. M. de Wolf, en date du 21 xbre, 1790, par leſquelles leurs dites Alteſſes Royales s'obligent ſolidairement pour le montant deſdites obligationes, conformément aux conditions repriſes dans l'acte d'autorisation, & qui sont annoncées par le prospectus.

III.

Un contrat dans les termes les plus forts & les plus obligatoires entre leurs dites Altesses Royales, les Seigneurs dépositaires ci-dessus mentionnés & les susdits banquiers, par lequel son Altesse Royale le Prince de Galles assigne en dépôt les revenus, prérogatives & généralement tous les émoluments de son Duché de Cornouaille, pour les employer aux fins designées par lesdits actes, & en conformité des conditions y reprises, auxquels lesdits Seigneurs depositaires s'obligent & s'engagent également de se conformer, & en cas du moindre défaut ils peuvent y être contraints par voie de justice.

IV.

Un contract dans la même forme & de la même force du précédent, par lequel son Altesse Royale le Prince de Galles assigne en dépôt auxdits Seigneurs ses appanages aux conditions & sous l'obligation & engagement des mêmes Seigneurs comme au contrat précedént.

V.

Un Contrat dans la même forme & de la même force des deaux précedents, par leguel son Altesse Royale le Duc d'York assigne en depôt les Revenus de l'Evéche d'Osnabrug aux conditions & sous l'obligation, & engagement des Seigneurs depositaires, comme aux contrats précédents,

VI.

Un Contrat dans la méme forme & de la méme force des trois précédents, par lequel

lequel Son Alteſſe Royale le Duc d'York aſſigne en dépôt ſes appanages aux conditions & ſous l'obligation & engagement des ſeigneurs depoſitaires, comme aux contrats précédents.

VII.

Un Contrat dans la même forme & de la même force des quatre précédents par lequel Son Alteſſe Royale le Duc de Clarence aſſigne en dépôt ſes appanages aux conditions & ſous l'obligation & engagement des ſeigneurs depoſitaires, comme aux contrats précédents.

VIII.

Une déclaration des hautes parties contractantes des fins, auxquelles les ſuſdits revenus aſſignés en dépôt par les cinq contrats précédents ſont deſtinés, & l'engagement obligatoire des Seigneurs depoſitaires de de ſe conformer aux conditions préſcrites & de ne point ſe deporter d'aucuns deſdits revenus qu'en faveur des préteurs enſuite des engagements contractés par l'acte d'autoriſation ci-deſſus cité ſub No. 1. les deux obligations ſolidaires ſub No. 2, & les cinq contrats d'aſſignation en dépôt ſub. No. 3 à 7.

IX.

Un modele de police, par laquelle les vies de leurs Alteſſes Royales ſeront aſſurées à leurs fraix par cinq Seigneurs de la plus haute qualité & fortune, ſavoir: le Duc de Portland, le Compte Fitzwilliam, *le Viſcompte Malmsbury*, Lord Robert Spencer & Sir Thomas Dundas, pour ceux des prêteurs qui voudront ſe faire aſſurer de cette maniere, le tout conformément aux engagements qui en ſont paſſés dans les actes & contrats ci-devant cités.

FINALEMENT.

Extracts de diverſes Lettres de Meſſrs. Vandemeulen & Jowatt de Londres, relatifs à la ſolidité & ſureté de cet emprunt.

Londres le 23 *Juillet*, 1790.

Nous avons eu un entretien avec Monſeigneur le Duc de Portland l'ami intime de Son Alteſſe Royale le Prince de Galles, & qui en cette qualité ſe charge du ſoin de cette affaire; circonſtance heureuſe pour les prêteurs! puiſqu'il eſt homme à qui l'honneur eſt plus cher que la vie, & qui par conſéquent ne s'intéreſſera jamais dans une affaire où il y auroit la moindre déception. Pour mettre cette affaire plus au clair, nous avons fait conſulter un de nos premiers juriſconſultes par rapport aux points, ſur leſquels vous nous avez demandé des renſeignements, vous trouverez

ci-inclus

ci-inclus ſon avis que nous vous envoyons en original, pour que vous puiſſiez le faire traduire chez vous, afin de vous en ſervir vis-à-vis de ceux, a qui vous allez propoſer l'emprunt en queſtion. S'il s'y trouve quelque choſe qu'on a de la peine a comprendre, le Colonel Frederick, qui eſt parti ce matin pour ſe rendre dans votre ville, pourra vous l'eclaircir. Vous y verrez, que rien n'empêche, que les Princes en queſtion ne puiſſent affecter leurs appanages. Enfin, Meſſieurs, d'apres ce que nous venons de vous dire, nous regardons cet emprunt comme des plus ſolides, & dans lequel nous ne balancerions pas d'intéreſſer nos plus intimes amis, &c.

Londres le 20 *Août* 1790.

LES princes affectent non ſeulement les revenus du Duché de Cornouaille & de l'Evêché d'Oſnabrug, mais auſſe leur divers

 appanages

appanages annuels, pour le rembourſement du capital avec les intérêts & aſſurances, c'eſt àdire que les revenus de Cornouaille & d'Oſnabrug enſemble avec les appanages annuels des trois princes en queſtion ſeront aſſignés à certains ſeigneurs en dépôt, non ſeulement afin de payer les intérêts & aſſurances, mais auſſi d'en deduire les ſommes qui manqueront pour rembourſement du capital aux époques préſcrites. Ainſi l'acte de ſeſſion deſdits revenus & l'acceptation d'iceux ſe fera par le même inſtrument, dans lequel ſeront detaillés les fins, aux quelles les revenus en queſtion ſont deſtinés, & les ſeigneurs en queſtion, en ſignant cet inſtrument s'obligent de s'y conformer, ou à défaut pourront y être contraints par voie de juſtice. Nous trouvons ces conditions bien juſtes & raiſonnables; & pour ce qui regarde la ſureté de la caution, qu'on propoſe de donnér il n'y a ſuivant nos idées rien

 a redire,

a redire, & nous en ſommes d'autant plus convaincus, que l'avocat que nous avons employé à dreſſer cette propoſition, eſt un de nos plus ſavants juriſconſultes & qui aura le ſoin de faire dreſſer les actes en queſtion, qui ſe feront dans la forme la plus exacte & obligatoire, dans le cas quæ l'emprunt ait lieu, &c.

Londres le 31 *Xbre*, 1790.

NOUS avons maintenant celui de vous remettre ſous ce pli modele de la police d'aſſurance ſur les vies de leurs Alteſſes Royales, & de vous annoncer en même tems les noms des perſonnes qui ſe chargeront de la ſomme, quil y aura à faire aſſurer, ſavoir.

Sa Grandeur le Duc de Portland,
Le Compte Fitzwilliam,
Le Viſcompte Malmſbury,
Lord Robert Spencer,
Sir Thomas Dundas.

On

On a fait faire ici le calcul de cette aſſurance, & on trouve que le riſque d'aſſurer ces trois vies l'un parmi l'autre ne vaut que 5 ou ¼ pour cent. ce qui a animé les cinq nobles perſonnes ci-deſſus detailleés de ſe charger de la ſomme entiere qu'il y aura à aſſurer & on peut bien compten d'êtra aſſuré de la maniere la plus ſolide, puiſque les bien-fonds de chaqu'un d'eux vont beaucoup au-delà de la totalité de l'emprunt, nous croyons donc que, d'après ce que nous venons de vous dire, & que le Colonel Frederick eſt en état de vous confirmer, que les Prêteurs, ou au moins la plus grande partie ſe contenterons de devenir eux-mêmes les aſſureurs. Nous avions eſpérér de pouvoir vous envoyer par ce courier les copies de tous les autres actes pour ſervir de nantiſſement aux préteurs, & à cet effet nous avions fait faire des copies, afin de vous les envoyer; mais le

notaire

notaire nous a fait dire, que par l'étendue de ces actes il sera de toute impossibilité de les collationer & de les certifier avant le départ du courier, mais vous pouvez compten que vous les recevrez par le courier prochain, aussi fermement que si vous les aviez déja en mains. Notre sieur Jowett vient de retourner ce moment d'un entretien, qui dura trois heures, avec Leurs Altesses Royales, Sa Grandeur le Duc de Portland, le Duc de Northumberland & toutes les personnes intéressées dans les actes en question, lesquels il a vu signer, sceller & passer avec toutes les formalités qu'exigent les loix de ce Paix. Il a emporté ces actes avec lui & nous les avons en garde vous pouvez donc messieurs, commencer à ouvrir l'Emprunt avec la plus grande confiance, rien ne manque pour la sécurité des Prêteurs, & quand même l'Emprunt seroit

pour

pour un Monarque, on ne pouroit ſe rendre plus ſecure, &c.

Londres le 4 *Janvier*, 1791.

VOUS ceſſerez meſſieurs d'être étonnés du retard qu'ont éprouvé les pieces, lorſque vous en aurez vu l'étendue ; nous pouvons vous dire ſans la moindre reſerve, que nous croyons ces pieces dreſſées dans la forme la plus ſolide & à tous égards conformes aux Loix de notre Pays, & pour plus de ſureté nous avons employé un de nos plus habiles procureurs, & après que ces pieces ont été dreſſées nous les avons fait examiner par les Sieurs Lowten, Baldwin & Adam, trois des plus célebres juriſconſultes de ce Pays, qui les ont unanimement approuvées vous verrez, meſſieurs à ces pieces, que rien ne peut être en meilleur ordre, que les nobles perſonnages en queſtion guarantiſſent leurs revenus francs d'aucune hypotheque ou engagement quelconque qui puisse les affecter joint à tout cela, le caractere des seigneurs depositaires ne permet pas de former le moindre soupçon, d'autant plus que les trois princes en question, leur ont confié la totalité de leurs revenus sans reserve. Enfin il est très certain, que cet emprunt, moyennant les pieces en question se fera sur un pied aussi solide que celui de quelque prince etranger que ce soit, nous le regardons même aussi solide que nos fonds publics, & si pareille opération étoit de notre but, nous ne balancerions un moment d'y verser nos deniers.

Londres le 21 *Janviers*, 1791.

NOUS devons vous observer encore, que ces appanages & ces revenus seront perçus par des seigneurs depositaires affranchis de toute hypotheque ou obstacle quelconque, & que ces seigneurs se sont obligés par acte en forme de ne les appliquer qu'aux fins proposées, ainsi rien ne peut ètre plus sûr, car tous les actes qui servent pour securité de l'emprunt, sont dréßes de la maniere la plus solide & exécutés avec toutes les formalités qu' exigent les loix de ce pays, suivant lesquelles l'enregistrement des actes n'est pas nécessaire pour les rendre obligatoires, ainsi si comme il vous plait nous faire croire, notre signature ait de l'influence sur votre place, vous pouvez certifier à vos capitalistes en notre nom, que les pieces sont toutes dans le meilleur ordre, & que, quand même ils fussent sur les lieux, ils ne pourroient se faire cautionner d'une maniere plus solide.

Le Soussigné Notaire admis au Conseil Souverain de Brabant residant à Anvers, ayant examiné les actes repris dans le Relevé ci-dessus, concernant la Levée de 3,600,000 florins de change pour compte

de

de Leurs Alteſſes Royales le Prince de Galles le Duc de York & le Duc de Clarence, declare de les avoir trouves conformes au dit Relevé & dans la maniere la plus obligatoire, & que les extraits des lettres de Meſſ. van der Meulen & Joett de Londres, ci-deſſus mentionnées, ſont conformes à leurs originaux quant aux extraits, fait à Anvers le 5 Faerieur, 1791.

Joan. G. DEELEN, Not. R.

TRANSLATION.

A Statement of the Letters and Deeds relating to the Loan of 3,600,000 Florins Exchange Money, on the Account of their Royal Highneſſes the Prince of Wales, the Duke of York, and the Duke of Clarence, of which 1,800,000 Florins are negociated at the Houſe of Jean E. Werbrouck, at Antwerp.

A POWER of authority, ſigned by their Royal Highneſſes and witneſſes, dated the 16th of November, 1790, by which they authorize Mr. Jean E. Werbrouck to open, upon their account in common, a loan of 3,600,000 florins exchange money, upon the conditions which have been detailed in the proſpectus already printed for this purpuſe, with a promiſe to aſſign in truſt their appanages of revenues into the hands of ſix Engliſh noblemen of the firſt diſtinction, and of the greateſt fortune, viz. the Duke of Portland, the Duke of Northumberland, the Earl Fitzwilliam, the Lords Southampton, Rawdon, and Malmſbury, which truſt the ſaid lords accept by a deed at the foot of this authority, and engage to employ the funds, which ſhall come into their hands by virtue of this deed of truſt, conformably to the purpoſes for which they [illegible]

1. For

1. For the half-yearly payment of the annual intereſt.

2. For the payment of the life inſurances hereafter ſtipulated.

3. For the annual reſervation of 3000l. to be employed in the conſolidated annuities of the Bank of England, in the joint names of his Grace the Duke of Portland, Mr. Jean E. Werbrouck, and Mr. Joſiah Jowett, to ſerve as a ſinking fund.

4. For the reſervation of the ſums neceſſary for the repayment of the capital at the period which ſhall be preſcribed.

II.

Two obligatory bonds, executed by their Royal Highneſſes, each for 1,800,000 florins,

florins, the one in favour of Mr. Jean E. Werbrouck, and the other in favour of Mr. C. J. M. de Wolf, dated the 21ſt of December, 1790, by which their ſaid Royal Highneſſes bind themſelves under the penalties of the bond, to the terms ſtipulated by the act of authority and announced in the proſpectus.

III.

A contract, in the ſtrongeſt and moſt obligatory terms, between their ſaid Royal Highneſſes, the lord truſtees named as above, and the ſaid bankers, by which his Royal Highneſs the Prince of Wales makes over in truſt the revenues, prerogatives, and generally all the emoluments of his Dutchy of Cornwall, to be employed to the purpoſes ſtated by the ſaid deeds, and in conformity to the conditions contained

in

in them, to which purposes the lords trustees oblige and engage themselves to perform; and in case of the least default, they can be compelled to it by law.

IV.

A contract of the same form and force with the preceding, by which his Royal Highness the Prince of Wales makes over in trust to the same lords his appenages upon the terms, and under the obligation and engagement of the same lords as in the preceding contract.

V.

A contract of the same form and of the same force with the two preceding, in which his Royal Highness the Duke of York makes over in trust his revenues of the Bishoprick of Osnaburg, upon the

terms,

terms, and under the obligation and engagement of the ſame lords truſtees as in the preceding contracts.

VI.

A contract of the ſame form, and of the ſame force with the three preceding, in which his Royal Highneſs the Duke of York makes over in truſt to the ſame lords his appanages, upon the terms, and under the obligation and engagement of the ſame lords truſtees as in the preceding contracts.

VII.

A contract of the ſame form, and of the ſame force with the four preceding, in which his Royal Highneſs the Duke of Clarence makes over in truſt to the ſame lords his appanages, upon the terms, and under the obligation and engagement of the ſame lords truſtees as in the preceding contracts.

VIII.

A declaration of the high contracting parties of the purpoſes to which the above revenues ſo made over in truſt, by the five preceding contracts are deſtined, and the obligatory bond of the lords truſtees, to conform to the preſcribed conditions, and not to apply any of the above revenues but in favour of the lenders, in virtue of the engagements contracted by the act of authority, N° I. by the two bonds N° II. and by the five contracts of aſſignment in truſt, N° III. IV. V. VI. and VII.

IX.

A model of a policy, by which the lives of their Royal Highneſſes are to be enſured

ſured by five noblemen of the higheſt rank and fortune, viz. the Duke of Portland, the Earl Fitzwilliam, *Le Viſcomte de Malmſbury*, Lord Robert Spencer, and Sir Thomas Dundas, for ſuch of the lenders as chuſe to be enſured in this manner, the whole conformable to the engagements taken in the acts and contracts abovementioned.

FINALLY.

Extracts of different letters of Meſſrs. Vander Meulen and Jowett of London, reſpecting the validity and ſecurity of this loan.

London, 23*d July*, 1790.

" WE have had an interview with his Grace the Duke of Portland, the intimate friend of his Royal Highneſs the Prince of Wales, and who in this capacity undertakes

takes the care of this bufinefs, a circumftance the moft happy for the lenders, becaufe he is a man whofe honour is dearer to him than his life, and who confequently will never engage in a bufinefs in which there is the leaft deception: to make the bufinefs clear, we have confulted one of our firft lawyers, on the points on which you had defired information: you will find enclofed the opinion, which we fend you in the original, in order that you may have it tranflated, in cafe you fhould wifh to make ufe of it with thofe to whom you mean to propofe the loan in queftion: if there is any thing which you have difficulty in underftanding, Colonel Frederick, who fet off this morning for your city, will explain it to you. You will fee that nothing hinders the Princes in queftion from pledging their appanages; and, in fine, from what we have ftated to you, we conſider this loan as one of the moſt ſolid nature, and one in which we would not heſitate to engage our beſt friends.

London, 20 *Auguſt*, 1790.

The Princes pledge, not only the revenues of the dutchy of Cornwall and the biſhoprick of Oſnaburg, but alſo their ſeveral annual appanages, for the repayment of the capital, with the intereſt and inſurances, that is to ſay, that the revenues of Cornwall and of Oſnaburg, together with the annual appanages of the three princes in queſtion, ſhall be made over to certain Lords in truſt, not only to pay the intereſt and inſurance, but alſo to deduct the ſums which will be wanted for the repayment of the capital, at the periods preſcribed, therefore the act of the transfer of theſe revenues, and of the acceptance by the truſtees, will be comprehended in the ſame inſtru-

inſtrument, in which the objects will be detailed for which thoſe revenues are deſtined, and the Lords in queſtion, by ſigning this inſtrument, oblige themſelves to conform to it, and in default may be compelled to it by due courſe of law. We think theſe conditions very juſt and reaſonable, and as to the validity of the ſecurity which they propoſe to give, we think that no objection can ariſe; and we are the more convinced of it, becauſe the lawyer whom we have employed to prepare this engagement is one of our ableſt counſellors, and he will take care to frame the deeds in queſtion in the moſt exact, and the moſt obligatory form, in caſe the loan takes place, &c.——

London 31 *Dec.* 1790.

" We ſend you under this cover, the model of the policy of inſurance on the lives

lives of their Royal Highneſſes, and the names of the perſons who will undertake for the ſum to be inſured, viz. his Grace the Duke of Portland, the Earl Fitzwilliam, *Les Viſcomte de Malmſbury*, Lord Robert Spencer, and Sir Thomas Dundas; we have here calculated this inſurance, and we find that the riſk of inſuring theſe three lives, one with another, is worth only five ſhillings, or $\frac{1}{4}$ *per cent.* which has encouraged the above five noble perſonages to charge themſelves with the entire ſum to be inſured, and you may depend upon being inſured in the manner the moſt ſecure, in as much as the property of each of them is very much larger than the whole of the loan; we, therefore, think, from what we have ſtated to you, and which Colonel Frederick is authoriſed to confirm to you, that the lenders, or at leaſt the greateſt part of them, will be contented to become their own inſurers.

We

We had hoped to have been enabled to ſend you by this courier, the copies of all the other acts, as a ſecurity for the lenders, and with this view we had ordered copies, in order to ſend them to you, but the notary has informed us, that from the ſize of theſe acts, it will be impoſſible to collate and certify them before the departure of the courier, but you may as certainly count upon receiving them by the next courier, as if you had them now in your hands. Our Mr. Jowett is this moment returned from an interview of three hours, with their Royal Highneſſes, his Grace the Duke of Portland, the Duke of Northumberland, and all the perſons intereſted in the acts in queſtion, which he has ſeen ſigned, ſealed, and delivered, with all the formalities required by the laws of this country; he has brought away theſe acts, and we have them in our cuſtody, you may therefore begin to open this loan with the greateſt confidence, as one in which nothing is wanting for the ſecurity of the lenders, and which could not be rendered more ſecure, even if it were for the public ſervice of a crowned head."

London, 4 *Jan*. 1791.

"You will not be ſurprized at the delay of theſe deeds when you have ſeen the ſize of them: we can now ſay, without the leaſt reſerve, that we believe them framed in the form the moſt ſolid, and in every way conformable to the laws of our country; for greater caution, we have employed one of our ableſt attorneys, and after they have been put into their proper ſhape, they were examined by Meſſrs. Lowten, Baldwin, and Adam, three of our moſt celebrated lawyers, who have unanimouſly approved them; you will, therefore, ſee by

theſe

these deeds, that nothing can be in better order; that the noble personages in question guaranty their revenues free from any incumbrance or engagement which may affect them; add to this, the character of the Lords Trustees does not admit of the smallest mistrust, the rather as these three princes have entrusted to them the whole of their revenues without reserve; in short, it is very certain that this loan, in consequence of this trust, will be as solid as that of any foreign prince whatsoever; we even consider it as solid as our public funds, and if this speculation lay in our line, we should not hesitate a moment to engage our property in it."

London, 21 *Jan.* 1791.

"We must observe to you, that these appanages and these revenues, will be received by the Lords Trustees, free from every incumbrance or engagement whatſoever; and that the Lords have obliged themſelves by formal deed, to apply them only to the purpoſes propoſed, ſo nothing can be more ſure, for all the acts for the ſecurity of this loan are framed in the moſt ſolemn manner, and executed with all the formalities required by the laws of this country, under which the regiſtry of deeds is not neceſſary to render them obligatory; therefore, if as you wiſh us to believe our name has any influence on your exchange, you may certify to your monied people, in our name, that theſe deeds are all in the beſt order, and that even if they were on the ſpot, they could not ſecure themſelves in a more ſolid manner.

The underſigned notary, admitted by the ſovereign council of Brabant, and reſiding

at

at Antwerp, having examined the acts referred to in this ſtatement, concerning the loan of 3,600,000 florins, exchange money, on account of their Royal Hignefſes the Prince of Wales, the Duke of York, and Duke of Clarence, declares he has found them conformable to the ſaid ſtatement, and in the moſt binding form, and that the extracts of letters from Meſſrs Vander Meulen and Jowett, of London, abovementioned, agree with the originals.

Antwerp, 15 *Feb.* 1791.

JOAN. G. DEELEN, Nots. Rs.

Theſe two papers have amongſt others been lately printed and diſperſed at Antwerp, and in other parts of the Dutch and Auſtrian Flanders, and have been reprinted in England. In commenting upon them, every reſpectful attention ſhould be obſerved to the three illuſtrious names brought forward to the public eye; nor can this matter be ſuppoſed to be unintereſting, or unfit for diſcuſſion, as it is the particular privilege of Engliſhmen to diſcuſs with gravity and decency, every public act involving the national credit, honour, or ſecurity; but upon this occaſion no difficulty occurs, as it will be plain, upon a full inveſtigation of the ſubject, that the papers carry with them the fulleſt refutation of any credit affected to be given to them, by the uſe of thoſe three reſpectable names, and of others, to whom their honour is ſtated "to be dearer than their "life, and who conſequently would not "be parties to any deception;" and it is equally certain that no Engliſh merchant or banker can have committed himſelf to his correſpondents, in the manner which theſe papers, unſigned and unauthenticated, ſuppoſe to have been the caſe, upon the

opinion

opinion of ſome *juriſconſulte*, whoſe name does not appear, and who probably never exiſted; as it will be ſufficiently obvious to the plaineſt comprehenſion, that the terms ſtated in theſe papers give to the lenders no legal ſecurity whatſoever, for one ſhilling advanced upon the revenues of the dutchy of Cornwall, or upon what is there termed the appanages of the three elder princes of our Royal Family; and a little conſideration will ſhew, that no Engliſh lawyer can have adviſed the loan of money, upon the ſecurity of the revenues of the biſhoprick of Oſnaburg, though that part of the queſtion is leſs intereſting to us, except as the unauthorized uſe of the name of the ſovereign of that principality, muſt excite our indignation againſt the compiler and publiſher of thoſe papers.

The propoſition, as it meets the eye, is ſimply this:—to raiſe for the uſe of their

Royal Highnesses the sum of 3,600,000 guilders (320,000l. sterling), by loan negociated with foreign bankers, for which a legal interest is assigned upon certain securities there stated, which are to be made over in *depositum* (trust) to five persons of the first distinction and property who are parties to the said deed, and engage to pay the interest, the insurance of their Royal Highnesses lives, and the sum of 3000l. annually into the English funds, on a trust vested in three other names, as a sinking-fund for the repayment of the principal money in 25 years. It is obvious that the first principle of this loan is, that the securities must continue in *statu quo* in the hands to which they are *made over in trust* for the full term of 25 years. If, therefore, the whole or any part of these securities are by law unalienable for any such purpose, or if they can be invalidated by any other accident ſave that which is guarded againſt by the inſurance of the life ſeparately of each of their Royal Highneſſes, or if the ſaid ſecurities, or any part of them be of a nature in which their Royal Highneſſes have no legal or veſted property whatſoever, it is clear that no "Juriſconſulte", no lawyer of credit, or merchant of character can (knowing theſe facts) recommend to monied men this loan, "as a concern equally ſolid with "the publick funds, and one in which "they ſhould be ready to engage their "own property."

I ſhall conſider this property ſo to be aſſigned, under its different heads.

DUTCHY OF CORNWALL.

This great and diſtinguiſhed fief is held under grants of a very ſingular nature,

and

and the profits of it arife under two general heads of revenue, feparately granted; viz. the Dutchy of Cornwall with the lands, manors, and land-profits of every fort; and, fecondly, the ftannaries or tin-mines, with the coinage or duty arifing from all tin raifed in Cornwall.

The grant of the firft is not to be found in the book to which I fhall have occafion frequently to refer, and which is in every publick and private collection; a book of the firft authority, becaufe it was compiled by our ableft antiquarian and hiftoriographer from the publick records, by authority; but this omiffion is immaterial, becaufe the original grant is recited in a fubfequent charter or confirmation fixty years afterwards, and the words of thefe grants will fufficiently fhew that the Dutchy and its profits were alienated from the

the Crown under ſtipulations, which make it impoſſible for the Duke of Cornwall to apply it to any other uſe whatſoever.

In the Fœdera conventiones literæ & acta publica Regum Angliæ, by Tho. Rymer.

Vol IV. P. 735.

Edwardus III.
17 March, 1337.

Pro Edwardo D. Cornubiæ de Stannariâ conceſſâ Rex Vice-Comite Cornubiæ,---

Recites the King's intention to diſtinguiſh his eldeſt ſon, and that he has created him Duke of Cornwall. " Et i er cæ-
" tera que eidem filio noſtro *pro ſtatu &*
" *honore Ducis decentius juxta generis ſui*
" *nobilitatem continendis & liberius ſuppor-*
" *tandis*, dedimus & conceſſimus pro nobis
" & hæredibus noſtris Stannariam noſtram
" in comitatu predicto una cum cunagio

 " ejuſdem

" ejuſdem Stannariæ, &c. Habendam &
" tenendam eidem duci & ipſius & hæ-
" redum ſuorum Regum Angliæ Filiis
" primogenitis & dicti loci ducibus in
" regno Angliæ hæreditarie ſucceſſuris,
" &c."

Teſte rege apud Weſtmonaſterium,
17° die Martis, per ipſum Regem
& totum conſilium in Parliamento.

The next charter which occurs is, from the ſame king upon the death of his ſon Edward Prince of Wales. He left a widow; the Princeſs Joan, who became, by common law, entitled to her third part of theſe poſſeſſions, as her dowry; which right this charter recognizes and ſecures, confirming, at the ſame time, the other two thirds to her young ſon, Richard Prince of Wales.

Vol. VII. P. 126.
20 Nov. 1376.

Edwardus III. Rex Vice Comiti & Eſcheatori Cornubiæ.

Commands inter alia the liberat or livery of two parts of the Dutchy of Cornwall to Richard, Prince of Wales, with reverſion of the third part after the death of his mother Joan, the widow of Edward, Prince of Wales. " Salvâ (Joannæ Predictæ) " dote ſuâ ipſam de fædis & advocationi- " bus prædictis ſecundum legem & con- " ſuetudinem regni noſtri Angliæ con- " tingente per nos aſſignandâ."

Teſte, &c.

The next Prince of Wales who occurs in our hiſtory is Henry, ſon to King Henry the Fourth; who, immediately upon his acceſſion, granted the following

 charter

charter, which recites the original charter from King Edward the Third to his ſon.

Vol. VIII. P. 91. 15 October, 1399. Henry IV. Rex Eſcheatori Cornubiæ.

Commands the livery of the Dutchy, &c. to Henry Prince of Wales, reciting the grant of his grandfather, Edward III. in theſe words: " Cum dominus Edwardus nuper Rex Angliæ Avus noſter " volens perſonam Edwardi filii ſui pri- " mogeniti honorare, &c. dederit ipſumque " in ducem Cornubiæ præfecerit: Ac pre- " dictus avus noſter omnia caſtra burgos " villas maneria honores Stannaria cunagia " firmas terras & tenementa ſimul cum " fœdis & advocationibus & omnibus aliis " ſupra dictis *eidem ducatui annexerit &* " *univerit in perpetuam remanſura. Ita* " *quod*

" *quod ab eodem ducatu aliquo tempore nulla*
" *tenus ſeparentur nec alicui nec aliquibus*
" *aliis quam dicti loci ducibus per ipſum*
" *avum noſtrum vel hæredes ſuos donentur*
" ſeu aliis ejuſdem loci decedentibus (ad
" quos ducatus prætextu dictæ conceſſionis
" præfati avi noſtri ſpectare dinoſcitur) tunc
" non apparentibus idem ducatus cum Caſ-
" tris Burgis villis & omnibus aliis ſu-
" pradictis ad ipſum avum noſtrum &
" hæredes ſuos Reges Angliæ revertantur
" in manibus ſuis & ipſorum hæredum
" ſuroum Regum Angliæ retinenda quouſ-
" que de hujus modi filio ſeu filius in
" dicto regno Angliæ hereditarie ſucceſ-
" ſuris apparent. Liberes habenda juxta
" tenorem & effectum cartæ ipſius avi noſ-
" ſupradictæ.

Teſte, &c.

No grant of livery appears to Henry, Prince of Wales, ſon to Henry the Vth, who was in France when his ſon was born, and died there before his ſon was nine months old.

Edward, Prince of Wales, ſon to Henry the VIth, was born during his father's inſanity in 1453; the livery of the Dutchy does not appear in Rymer, but it is referred to as having taken place under King Edward's charter, by the following writ:

Vol. XI. Page 385, 28 Jan. 1457. Hen. 6tus. Rex. Arch. Eboracenſi & aliis.

Appoints them tutors to his ſon, pro gubernatione, &c. ducatus.

Teſte, &c.

From

From this period it ſeems unneceſſary to quote more charters in proof of the fact, that the eldeſt ſon to the King of England holds the Dutchy of Cornwall under the charter of Edward III. but it is material to conſider the treaties between King Henry the VIIth, and Ferdinand of Spain, for the marriage of Arthur, Prince of Wales, to the Princeſs, Katharine.

Vol. XII. P. 461, 22 Nov. 1491.
Vol. XII. P. 517, 8 March, 1492.
Vol. XII. P. 658, 18 June, 1497.

In all of which the King is made a party to the aſſignment of a Dowry which Ferdinand did not chuſe to truſt to the operation of our common law, but ſtipulated that the ſaid Princeſs " dotabitur per prædictum
" Regem

" Regem Angliæ & Arthurum, P. Walliæ, " in tertia parte Ducatus Cornubiæ, &c." and accordingly we find,

Vol. XII. P. 780, 14 Nov. 1501. Pro Katherina Hispaniæ aſſignatio dotis Arthurus, P. Walliæ, &c. Salutem,

Recites all theſe treaties, and proceeds, " de expreſſa voluntate conceſſu aſſenſu ac " mandato ejuſdem illuſtriſſimi Regis & " Patris noſtri metuendiſſimi dotamus," &c. to aſſign particular lands, parcel of the Dutchy of Cornwall, as her dower. It ſhould ſeem, therefore, that an aſſignment could not be made by his own authority, without the conſent of his father as a party, to this alienation of the ſpecifick lands aſſigner as a dower. She outlived her firſt huſband and remarried with Henry, P. of Wales, when the ſame proceedings took

 place,

place, respecting the lands assigned for dower, she having previously resigned her claim to them as Prince Arthur's widow, as recited by —

Vol. XIII. P. 76, Anno 1503. Confirmatio tractatus de matrimonio H. Principis Walliæ cum Katherinâ Infante.

From this period no Prince of Wales has intermarried until Frederick Louis, P. of Wales, married the Princess of Saxe Gotha: no dowry was settled upon her; the bill passed in the 10th year of the late King, cap. 29, only enabling the King to grant her an *annuity* in the contingency of the Prince's death, in consequence of which she became entitled to her third part, by common law, of the Dutchy of Cornwall, and enjoyed to her death a further annuity of 10,000 l. which she accepted in lieu of that third part, for which she executed a

 release

releaſe by proper inſtrument, in the firſt year of his preſent Majeſty.

From all theſe documents theſe concluſions are incontrovertible.

I.

That the Duke of Cornwall holds the ſaid Dutchy by the charter, and under the very particular limitations of King Edward the third.

II.

That the ſaid Dutchy being granted for the ſupport of the dignity of the eldeſt ſon of the King, and under the expreſs ſtipulation that " the parts of it are annexed and " united to remain for ever, ſo as never to " be ſeparated at any time and in any man- " ner," cannot be transferred into the legal poſſeſſion of any other perſon, or made over

in

in truſt, even during the life of the Duke, for the payment of any ſum whatſoever.

III.

That if the Duke of Cornwall intermarries and dies, his widow would become entitled, by common law, ſanctioned by the direct precedents above-quoted from the oldeſt period to the preſent times, to one-third of the whole Dutchy.

IV.

That if the Duke of Cornwall having married has a ſon, that ſon, upon his father's ſucceſſion to the Crown of England, is entitled to the Dutchy.

V.

That if the Duke of Cornwall ſucceeds to the Crown of England, and, either married or unmarried, has no ſon, the Dutchy of

Cornwall is veſted in the Crown until the birth of ſuch ſon; and, being veſted in the Crown, is ſubject to the controul of Parliament.

The two firſt poſitions ſtrike at the very principle of the loan ſtated in this paper; and if they are clearly made out, the five names ſtated to be Truſtees would be amenable to the law for profeſſing to undertake ſuch a truſt; nor could they diſcharge the firſt and moſt ſacred duty of Truſtees, by holding it for the benefit of the creditors againſt the borrower, if the borrower, by neglect, or by any other circumſtance, which the law, and the very tranſaction, always preſumes to be poſſible, ſhould be in arrear for the intereſt, or for the inſurance of lives, or for the payment towards the Sinking Fund; ſtill leſs can they engage to hold for 25 years, the revenues which are

not,

not, and cannot, be enſured againſt any one of the contingencies ſtated in the 3d, 4th, and 5th poſitions; and conſequently no merchant, or lawyer, is juſtified in ſtating that, "this loan is conformable to the laws "of the land;" or in recommending his correſpondents "to engage in ſuch a loan "with the greateſt confidence, as one in "which nothing is wanted for the ſecurity "of the lenders, and which could not be "rendered more ſecure even if it were for "the publick ſervice of a crowned head.

The next property ſtated in theſe unauthorized papers to be aſſigned, is the appanage of each of the three Princes.

A very few words will diſmiſs this ſecurity, for (with the exception of the Dutchy of Cornwall granted to the Prince of Wales) the ſons of the King of England have no appanage,

appanage, or property, nor any income whatſoever, ſave what it has pleaſed their father to allow them annually out of his Civil Liſt, or eſtabliſhment, during his Royal pleaſure; and it is wholly in his power (never having made any legal or permanent grant to any of his ſons, or even by law able to make any) to encreaſe, diminiſh, or totally to withhold the allowance which he now makes, in ſuch proportions as he thinks proper to every one of them.

The commoneſt and loweſt attorney would be hooted out of ſociety who could adviſe a client to lend his money upon ſuch ſecurity; and conſequently no merchant, or lawyer, is juſtified in ſtating to his correſpondents, that " nothing hinders the " Princes in queſtion from pledging their " appanages; and that this loan is one of " the moſt ſolid nature, and one in which

" they would not hefitate to engage their
" beft friends."

The laft property ftated in thefe unauthorized papers to be affigned is, the Bifhoprick of Ofnaburg.

On this head I feel but little intereft, excepting to prove, from the impoffibility of fuch a truft being conveyed, or executed, that it is equally impoffible that the refpectable name in queftion can have made over, or that five gentlemen, " whofe honour is " dearer than their lives," can have undertaken to receive the transfer of thefe revenues in *depofitum* (truft) and to hold the collection of them as by their duty (if the truft is not a mockery) they are bound to do, againft the Sovereign for the creditor.

I do not know very deeply the civil law or the peculiar law of the empire binding upon every member of it, but from the plaineſt and firſt principles of it, and from ſeveral examples in our days, *one exiſting at this moment*, I do not heſitate to affirm, that the Directors and Co-eſtates of the Circle are the only Truſtees whom the Chamber of Wetzlaer would authorize to execute ſuch a truſt; and that by the Germanic law, no alien, no foreigner, not ſubject of the empire, can hold any truſt of fiefs, or lands, ſubject to the ſervice to which all ſuch lands are engaged; ſtill leſs can he hold in truſt the revenues of a great principality for a debt contracted for purpoſes not known or recognized by the States of that Biſhoprick: One of theſe Directors of the Circle of Weſtphalia, and not the leaſt important, is the King, Elector of Hanover, who is not ſtated in theſe papers

to

to be a party to this tranſaction: but a decisive objection to this ſecurity ariſes from the nature of theſe revenues, which conſiſt of a vaſt variety of ſmall duties, and of large voluntary contributions, ſubject, with a very few exceptions, to the controul of the States of the Biſhoprick, who have hitherto, with chearfulneſs, paid largely to the honorable ſupport of their Sovereign, but are not ſtated to be parties to this tranſaction; and moſt certainly cannot be controuled as to the quantum which they may think proper to grant to him, or to the terms under which they may grant it, by five Engliſh gentlemen perfectly unknown to that country and to its conſtitution: and conſequently no merchant, or lawyer, is juſtified in ſtating, "that theſe Princes "have entruſted to the Lords, who are Truſ-"tees, the whole of their revenues, and in "recommending this Loan as being, in

" consequence of such a Trust, as solid as
" that of any foreign Prince whatsoever,
" or even as solid as the publick funds."

But these licentious papers, in their use of the first names in this country, without authority, and pledging no signature as vouching for their various details, give an additional proof against themselves, by attempting to cure every objection of the most serious nature, arising out of the laws, customs, and constitution of Great Britain and Germany, by a general reference to five names, as persons who have undertaken the trust, and who thereby give to the borrower the most solid security, " in-
" asmuch as the property of each of them
" is very much larger than the whole
" amount of the loan." It would be invidious to detect this misrepresentation by specific investigation of each of the

names

names there ſtated, but it is notorious that the firſt properties in England are uſually entailed to various uſes upon the marriage of the parties, and that a tenant for life can give no ſecurity which can affect ſuch an eſtate: this obſervation attaches upon three of theſe diſtinguiſhed perſonages. No ſuch perſon as "Le Viſcompte de Malmſbury" exiſts, and the youngeſt brother of the Duke of Marlborough would ſmile at ſeeing the proviſion which was made for him by the will of Sarah Dutcheſs of Marlborough, magnified to 320,000l. if he did not feel (what I am perſuaded will be his firſt emotion) the warmeſt indignation at the attempt to make ſuch a uſe of his name. And the public remember, with ſuch deep impreſſions of gratitude, the manly and conſtitutional negative to the idea of an encreaſe of the Prince of Wales's allowance, which every one believes to have been given in 1787, and more decidedly in 1789, by Lord Fitzwilliam and the Duke of Portland, (whoſe honour that paper ſtates to be dearer to him than his life) that they will reject with indignation every inſinuation that his Lordſhip, and ſtill more ſo that his Grace, has been privy, much leſs a party to ſuch a tranſaction.

But the ſtrongeſt ſecurity to the public againſt theſe anonymous papers is founded on the ſolemn pledge given through the King, his father, to both houſes of Parliament, by the firſt of the reſpectable names ſo indecently brought forward to the public eye. It is, therefore, the duty of every Engliſhman to reſcue him from ſuch an imputation, by repeating to the world that engagement, which every perſon in this iſland joined to applaud. His Royal Highneſs certainly knew the difficulties which

pre-

presented themselves to his father, in recurring for the payment of a very heavy debt to the affection and generosity of Parliament; for these impressions were conveyed in terms the most honourable to our Sovereign, and to his faithful Commons, in his message* on the 21st May, 1787, in which his Majesty states, that "he "could not expect or desire the assistance "of this House, but on a well-grounded "expectation, that the Prince will avoid "contracting any debts in future; that "with a view to this object, and from an "anxious desire to remove any possible "doubt of the sufficiency of the Prince's "income, to support amply the dignity of "of his situation, his Majesty has directed "a sum of 10,000l. *per annum*, to be paid "out of his civil list, in addition to the "*allowance* which his Majesty has hitherto

* Vide Commons Journals.

" given him; and his Majeſty has the " ſatisfaction to inform the Houſe, *that " the Prince of Wales has given his Ma- " jeſty the fulleſt aſſurance of his determina- " tion to confine his future expences within " his income.*"

This ſolemn and explicit pledge was received and recognized by the Houſe of Commons in their Addreſs of the 24th May, as the ground of their vote of the very heavy ſum in diſcharge of His Royal Highneſs's debt; for after expreſſing " their gratitude to the King, for making " an additional allowance to remove every " poſſible doubt of the ſufficiency of His " Highneſs's income, and after teſtifying " the greateſt ſatisfaction in hearing that " His Royal Highneſs has given to His " Majeſty the fulleſt aſſurances of his firm " determination to confine his future ex- " pences

" pences within his income," they add, " that *in full reliance on the assurances which* " *His Majesty has received*, they humbly " desire His Majesty to issue the sum re- " quired, and pledge themselves to make " good the same."

It is impossible to read this memorable engagement without feeling with the greatest sensibility for the honour of his Royal Highness, so deeply wounded by these anonymous papers circulated through-out the continent, and re-published in England; for it is not possible for imagination to conceive that any person can so far have forgotten the pledge given by His Royal Highness as to advise him to contract, by this loan, such a debt as the enormous sum of 320,000l.; and if any person could advise it, His Royal Highness knows so well the duties he owes to the laws, to his father, to his character, and to the high station in which he is placed, that he could not entertain, for a moment, so pernicious a counsel; for he well knows that those laws would attach very severely upon such a loan, even if objections had not occurred to its validity; for God forbid! that the Prince or King of England can, for an immediate loan of money, unknown to and unauthorized by Parliament, transfer those funds *which are granted to them for the honourable support of that dignity* entrusted to them by the publick. If then these anonymous and injurious libels have not been yet prosecuted by those whose bounden duty directs them to protect the character and honour of their Royal Master, by recurring to the courts of law on such occasions; I am persuaded that they were prevented from following the dictates of their feelings and

of

of their judgment, by the peculiar delicacy of their ſituation, in coming forward to proſecute, in the name of His Royal Highneſs, a libel which has taken the indecent liberty of adding their names (certainly unauthorized) to the liſt of perſons ſtated in theſe papers as parties to this negociation.

But the reparation which the law can give to theſe Royal Perſonages, and to the other reſpectable names ſtated in theſe papers, can in part be made by the public diſbelief and diſavowal of this tranſaction; inaſmuch as it militates againſt every profeſſion or duty to which, in their different ſtations, the parties ſtand pledged; and inaſmuch as the whole tranſaction is of a nature that can give no ſecurity to the creditor, and conſequently would reflect the highest disgrace on the parties to it, if it had not been palpably clear from the considerations which I have urged, that the whole of these papers is unvouched, unauthorized, and destitute of any foundation whatsoever.

F I N I S.

NEW BOOKS,

LATELY PUBLISHED BY

JOHN STOCKDALE, PICCADILLY.

1. A Voyage round the World, but more particularly to the North-Weſt Coaſt of America, the great Mart of the Fur Trade. Embelliſhed with Forty-two Charts, Views, and other Copper-plates, repreſenting the Diſcoveries. Dedicated, by Permiſſion, to his Majeſty, Sir Joſeph Banks, Bart. and the Lords of the Admiralty; by Captains Portlock and Dixon. In two Vols. 4to. Price in Boards 2l. 6s.—Or fine Paper, with the Natural Hiſtory, coloured, 3l. 3s.

2. The Voyage of Governor Phillip to Botany-Bay; with an Account of the Eſtabliſhment of the Colonies at Port Jackſon and Norfolk Iſland: Compiled from Authentic Papers, which have been received from the ſeveral Departments. To which are added, the Journals of Lieut. Shortland of the *Alexander*; Lieut. Watts of the *Penrhyn*; Lieut. Ball of the *Supply*; and Capt. Marſhall of the *Scarborough*; with an account of their new Diſcoveries. The Maps and Charts taken from actual Surveys, and the Plans and Views drawn on the Spot, by Capt. Hunter, Lieut. Shortland, Lieut. Watts, Lieut. Dawes, Lieut. Bradley, Capt. Marſhall, &c. and engraved by Medland, Sherwin, Mazell, Harriſon, &c. Inſcribed, by Permiſſion, to the MARQUIS of SALISBURY. In one large Volume Quato, printed on fine Paper, and embelliſhed with Fifty-five fine Copper-plates; Second Edition, in Boards 1l. 11s. 6d.

The following is a Liſt of the Engravings which are in this Work.

1 Head of Governor Phillip, from a Painting in the Poſſeſſion of Mr. Nepean, by F. Wheatley; engraved by Sherwin

2 Head of Lieut. Shortland, engraved by Sherwin, from a Painting of Shelley's

3 Head of Lieut. King, from a Painting by Wright

4 View of Botany Bay, with the Supply and Sirius at Anchor, and the Tranſports coming in

5 A large Chart of Port Jackſon

6 A View in Port Jackſon, with the Natives in their Canoes trouling

7 View of the Natives in Botany Bay

8 Map of Lord Howe Iſland, and View of ditto

9 Head of Lieut. Watts, drawn by Shelley, and engraved by Sherwin

10 View of Natives and a Hut in New South Wales

11 View of New South Wales

12 A large Plan of the Eſtabliſhment at Sydney Cove, Port Jackſon
13 A large Chart of Norfolk Iſland
14 View of Ball's Pyramid
15 Chart of Lieutenant Shortland's Diſcoveries
16 Track of the Alexander from Port Jackſon to Batavia
17 Chart of Capt. Marſhall's New Diſcoveries
18 View of the Natives in their ſailing Canoe at Mulgrave Iſlands
19 View of Curtis's Iſland
20 View of Macauley's Iſland
21 Caſpian Tern
22 The Kangaroo
23 The Spotted Opoſſum
24 Vulpine Opoſſum
25 Norfolk Iſland Flying Squirrel
26 Blue-bellied Parrot
27 Tabuan Parrot
28 Pennanthian Parrot
29 Pacific Parrot
30 Sacred King's Fiſher
31 Superb Warbler, male
32 Superb Warbler, female
33 Norfolk Iſland Petrel
34 Bronze-winged Pigeon
35 White-fronted Hern
36 Wattled Bee-eater
37 Pſittaceous Hornbill
38 Martin Cat
39 Kangaroo Rat
40 A Dog of New South Wales
41 The Black Cockatoo
42 Red-ſhouldered Paraquet
43 Watts's Shark
44 The Laced Lizard
45 New Holland Goat Sucker
46 White Gallinule
47 New Holland Caſſowary
48 Port Jackſon Shark
49 Yellow Gum Plant
50 Axe, Baſket, and Sword
51 Bag-throated Baliſtes
52 Fiſh of New South Wales
53 Great Brown King's Fiſher
54 Black Flying Opoſſum
55 Skeleton of the Head of a Kangaroo and Vulpine Opoſſum

N. B. A few of the Firſt Edition, with fine Impreſſions, and the Natural Hiſtory, beautifully coloured, may be had of Mr. Stockdale, price 2l. 12s. 6d. boards.

3. A Third Edition of Governor Phillip's Voyage, is elegantly printed in One large Volume, Royal Octavo, containing the whole of the Letter-Preſs, with the following Copper-plates. Price 10s. 6d. in boards.

1 Frontiſpiece, Head of Governor Phillip
2 Title-Page, with a beautiful Vignette
3 View of Botany Bay
4 View in Port Jackſon
5 Natives of Botany Bay
6 Map of Norfolk Iſland
7 Lieutenant King
8 View of a Hut in New South Wales
9 View in New South Wales
10 Sketch of Sydney Cove
11 Kangaroo
12 Spotted Opoſſum
13 Vulpine Opoſſum
14 Black Flying Opoſſum
15 Great Brown King's Fiſher
16 Bronze-winged Pigeon
17 New Holland Caſſowary
18 Lieutenant Shortland
19 Canoe and Natives in Mulgrave Range
20 Lieutenant Watts

4. Shakspeare, with a complete Index, Patronized by his Majeſty, and his Royal Highneſs the Prince of Wales. In one large Volume Octavo, beautifully printed on a fine Royal Paper, and embelliſhed with a Head of the Author,

thor, from the original Folio Edition; Price 1l. 11s. 6d. in Boards.

This beautiful Edition of SHAKSPEARE includes the Whole of his Dramatic Works; with Explanatory Notes, compiled from various Commentators. To which is added, a Copious Index to all the remarkable Passages and Words. By the Rev. SAMUEL AYSCOUGH, F. S. A.

N. B. For the Convenience of Ladies and Gentlemen who may think this Volume too large, a second Volume Title is printed, and a Title to the Index; so that the Purchaser may either bind the above Work in One, Two, or Three Volumes.

*** The Purchasers of the former Edition, may have the Index separate, consisting of near 700 Pages, Price 18s. in boards, or One Guinea, Calf gilt.

5. A splendid Demy Octavo Edition of ROBINSON CRUSOE.

This Day is published, beautifully printed on a fine Paper, in Two handsome Volumes, Demy Octavo, Price Eighteen Shillings in Boards, and embellished with Fifteen Original Engravings, and Two elegant Vignettes; the whole designed by STODHART, and engraved by MEDLAND: The Life and surprising adventures of ROBINSON CRUSOE; To which is added, The Life of DANIEL DE FOE. By GEORGE CHALMERS, Esq.

N. B. The Public will please to Order that Printed for Mr. Stockdale, as the Plates alone are worth more than the Price of the whole Book.

*** A few Copies of the first Impression, in two large Volumes, Royal Octavo, may be had of Mr. Stockdale, Price 1l. 1s. in Boards, or 1l. 7s. elegant Calf gilt.

The following is the subject of the Plates—With a Reference to the Work.

Plate I.—Title Page to Vol. I. with a beautiful Vignette, composed of the Wreck of a Ship.—Subject of Plate II.—Frontispiece to Vol. I.—Robinson Crusoe taking leave of his Father and Mother.—"My Father was a wise and grave Man; gave me serious and excellent Counsel against what he foresaw was my Design. He called me one Morning into his Chamber, where he

was

was confined by the Gout, and expoftulated very warmly with me upon this fubject." See page 2.

Subject of Plate III.—Robinfon Crufoe Shipwrecked and clinging to a Rock.—" I recovered a little before there turn of the Wave; and feeing I fhould be covered again with the Water, I refolved to hold faft by the piece of the Rock." See page 56.

Subject of Plate IV.—Robinfon Crufoe upon his Raft.—" Having plundered the Ship of what was portable and fit to hand out, I began with the Cables; and cutting the great Cable in pieces, fuch as I could move, I got two Cables and a Hawfer on Shore, with all the Iron-work could get; and having cut down the Sprit-fail-yard, and the Mizen-yard, and every thing I could to make a large Raft, I loaded it with all the heavy Goods, and came away." See page 69.

Plate V.—Robinfon Crufoe at work in his Cave.—" I made abundance of Things even without Tools, and fome with no more Tools than an Adze and a Hatchet, which, perhaps, were never made before, and that with infinite Labour." See Page 84.

Plate VI.—Robinfon Crufoe difcovers the Print of a Man's Foot.—" I was exceedingly furprifed with the Print of a Man's naked Foot on the Shore, which was very plain to be feen in the Sand. I ftood like one thunderftruck, or as if I had feen an Apparition; I liftened, I looked round me, I could hear nothing, nor fee any thing." See Page 194.

Plate VII.—Robinfon Crufoe firft fees and refcues his Man Friday.—" Having knocked this Fellow down, the other who purfued him ftopped, as if he had been frightened; and I advanced apace towards him; but as I came nearer, I perceived prefently he had a Bow and Arrow, and was fitting it to fhoot at me; fo I was then neceffitated to fhoot at him firft, which I did, and killed him at the firft Shot." See Page 256.

Plate VIII.—Robinfon Crufoe and Friday making a Boat.—" I fhewed him how to cut it out with Tools, which, after I had fhewed him how to ufe, he did very readily; and in about a Month's hard Labour we finifhed it, and made it very handfome." See Page 287.

Plate IX.—Robinfon Crufoe and Friday making a Tent to lodge Friday's Father and the Spaniard.—" Friday

and

and I carried them up both together between us; but, when we got to the outside of our Wall or Fortification, we were at a worse Loss than before, for it was impossible to get them over: and I was resolved not to break it down, so I set to work again, and Friday and I, in about two Hours Time, made a very handsome Tent, covered with old Sails, and above that with Boughs of Trees." See Page 304.

Plate X,—Title to Vol. II. with a beautiful Vignette, composed of Robinson Crusoe's Implements of Husbandry.

Plate XI.—Frontispiece.—Robinson Crusoe's first Interview with the Spaniards on his second Landing.—"First he turned to me, and pointing to them said, These, Sir, are some of the Gentlemen who owe their Lives to you; and then turning to them, and pointing to me, he let them know who I was; upon which they all came up one by one, not as if they had been Sailors, and ordinary Fellows, and I the like, but really as if they had been Ambassadors or Noblemen, and I a Monarch or a great Conqueror." See Page 42.

Plate XII.—The Plantation of the Two Englishmen.—"The two Men had innumerable young Trees planted about their Hut, that when you came to the Place nothing was to be seen but a Wood; and though they had the Plantation twice demolished, once by their own Countrymen, and once by the Enemy, as shall be shewn in its Place; yet they had restored all again, and every Thing was flourishing and thriving about them." See Page 90.

Plate XIII.—Tht two Englishmen retreating with their Wives and Children.—"Now, having great Reason to believe that they were betrayed, the first Thing they did was to bind the Slaves which were left, and cause two of the three Men, whom they brought with the Women, who, it seems, proved very faithful to them, to lead them with their two Wives, and whatever they could carry away with them, to their retired Place in the Woods. See Page 95.

Plate XIV.—The Spaniards and Englishmen burning the Indian Boats.—"They went to work immediately with the Boats; and getting some dry Wood together from a dead Tree, they tried to set some of them on fire, but they were so wet that they would scarce burn; however,

ever, the Fire so burned the upper Part, that it soon made them unfit for swimming in the Sea as Boats. See Page 113.

Plate XV.—Robinson Crusoe distributing Tools of Husbandry among the Inhabitants.—" I brought them out all my Store of Tools, and gave every Man a digging Spade, a Shovel, and a Rake, for we had no Harrows or Ploughs; and to every separate Place a Pick-axe, a Crow, and a broad Axe, and a Saw." See Page 134.

Plate XVI.—A View of the Plantation of the three Englishmen.—" Upon this he faced about just before me, as he walked along, and putting me to a full Stop, made me a very low Bow; I most heartily thank God and you, Sir, says he, for giving me so evident a Call to so blessed a Work." See Page 151.

Plate XVII.—Head of De Foe to face the Title of the Life.

*** That those Ladies and Gentlemen who have not had an Opportunity of seeing this Work, may form some Idea of the Execution and Elegance of the Engravings, Mr. STOCKDALE assures them it has cost him near Seventeen Hundred Pounds.

6. Stockdale's London Calendar for 1791. Complete with the Arms of the Peers, &c. The London Calendar, or Court and City Register, for England, Scotland, Ireland, America, and the East Indies, for 1791.

N. B. The Calendar separate, Price bound	0	2	0
or with an Almanack —	0	2	10
Ditto with Companion — —	0	4	6
Ditto with Companion, Bengal Calendar, and Almanack — —	0	6	6
Ditto with Companion, Bengal Calendar, Almanack, and Arms, complete	0	8	6
Ditto extra bound in Morocco —	0	13	6
7. Bengal Calendar for 1791 —	0	2	0

8. The Letters of Simkin the Second, Poetic Recorder of all the Proceedings upon the Trial of Warren Hastings, Esq; in Westminster-Hall. A New Edition, in one large Vol. Octavo. Price in Boards, 7s.

9. Simkin's Letters for 1790, to complete the first Edition. Boards, 3s.

SONGE
D'UN ANGLAIS,
FIDÉLE
À SA PATRIE,
ET
À SON ROI.

TRADUIT DE L'ANGLAIS.

A LONDRES:

Et se vend chez M. ELMSLEY, *Strand.*

M DCC. XCIII.

SONGE D'UN ANGLAIS,

Fidèle à ſa Patrie *&* *à ſon* Roi.

UN Romain, dans le temps où les Romains étaient eſclaves, *rêva* qu'il tuait le Tyran ; ce tyran le ſçut, & le fit punir de mort. J'ai *rêvé* que j'étais appelé aux Conſeils d'un bon Roi, d'un Roi qui a mérité de préſerver notre Conſtitution par ſes vertus, autant que notre Conſtitution le préſerve par ſes loix : j'eſpère que mon zèle, fût-il indiſcret, obtiendra au moins ſon indulgence ; je me fais un devoir égal, & de taire mon nom, & de publier mon Songe.

Il n'y a pas long-temps que je ſuis de retour dans ma patrie ; je ſoupirais après des loix & après des hommes. Perdu dans un voyage long & dangereux, j'ai erré au milieu d'un Peuple ſauvage, qui n'a d'autres règles que l'inſtinct de ſa férocité, qui adore le mauvais principe, & ne reconnaît pas une Divinité bienfaiſante ; qui lui ſacrifie des victimes humaines, & qui ſe nourrit de ſang humain. Echappé par un hafard miraculeux, & à leur facrifices, & à leurs feftins, en débarquant en Angleterre, je me fuis profterné, & j'ai baifé ce fol Britannique, où l'humanité la fageffe, la liberté, font des plantes indigènes. Tout-à-coup j'ai appris que la paix & les loix y étaient menacées; j'ai appris par qui & pourquoi elles l'étaient: j'ai frémi. Heureufement des Proclamations également fermes & prudentes, font venues ramener les bons, & frapper les méchans d'effroi. J'ai été fier de ma patrie, en voyant de toutes parts ces nobles Affociations qui fe formaient pour défendre les Loix, le Roi, & le Peuple. Je me fuis mêlé à la foule: beaucoup ont furpaffé mes lumières, aucun n'a furpaffé mon zèle. Abfent depuis long-temps de mon pays, j'avais de longs arrérages & une bien ancienne dette à lui payer. Le hafard a favorifé mes recherches, & je crois que peu de mes compatriotes en ont fu plus que moi fur les confpirations extérieures & internes. Ç'a été un grand jour pour l'Angleterre que le 13 Décembre, l'entrevue du Roi & du Peuple dans la Capitale de l'Empire, l'entoufiafme qui l'a fignalée, & l'ouverture du Parlement le plus patriotique, peut-être, qui fe foit encore tenu en Angleterre. Ç'a été un fpectacle confolant dans les deux Chambres, que cette lutte fi inégale de l'Ambition contre le Patriotisme, & d'une Rhétorique séditieuse contre l'Eloquence de la Vertu ; j'en ai été l'heureux témoin. Enfin, le 15, j'étais à la Chambre des Communes ; j'en croyais à peine mes oreilles lorsque j'entendais proposer de reconnaître *la République Française, & d'envoyer un Chargé d'Affaires à Paris, comme on en envoie un à Constantinople, & à Alger.* La forme même de cette proposition ne me réconciliait pas avec le fonds. Je conjurais la nature, toutes les fois qu'elle crée des talens si sublimes, de mettre à côté tout ce qui est nécessaire pour qu'on les bénisse toujours, & qu'on ne les redoute jamais. J'étais agité ; je m'unissais à la vertueuse indignation du Noble Lord qui demandait, *Comment on osait proposer au Parlement Anglais de s'associer à une bande de Voleurs & d'Assassins ?* En rentrant chez moi j'ai trouvé *l'acte énonciatif des crimes de Louis XVI.* La bétise de cet acte m'a plus inquiété que n'aurait fait sa malice. Quand on a le front de produire, contre un Roi, un tel acte d'accusation, il faut qu'on soit déterminé à voler dans les poches, & à assassiner sur les grand'routes ; par conséquent, ni conscience, ni pudeur, ni frein. Je me suis répété cette phrase de M. Burke : *Le Roi de France est jugé maintenant par le Citoyen Paine, qui sera jugé, dans peu de jours, par le Roi d'Angleterre,* (&

qui, ſi juſtice ſe fait, ſera pilorié, du moins en effigie). Je me ſuis rappelé une autre phraſe de la ſeconde Lettre du même M. Burke, ſur la Révolution Française, & je me ſuis demandé ſi le ſalut du Roi de France, auquel tient peut-être le ſalut de l'Europe, n'était pas un objet auſſi digne de l'attention des Cabinets, que la balance entre la Ruſſie & la Porte, ou bien entre la Pruſſe & l'Autriche. Au milieu de toutes ces agitations, j'ai cédé à la nature; car depuis trois nuits je n'avais pas dormi. Les mêmes penſées m'ont ſuivi dans le ſommeil; tout-à-coup un ſonge m'a tranſporté au Palais de St. James: Sa Majeſté y tenait Conſeil; on y avait appelé un député de chacune des Aſſociations formées dans chaque paroiſſe de Londres: celle dont je ſuis membre m'avait nommé ſon repréſentant, comme ayant une connaiſſance plus détaillée des complots. Chaque député a expoſé tout ce que, dans ſon arrondiſſement, on avait recueilli de faits & de preuves. Les Miniſtres ont opiné: pendant qu'ils parlaient, j'admirais en eux un vrai patriotiſme, un ferme attachement à la Conſtitution de leur pays, une fidélité inébranlable à leurs alliés; la juſte appréhenſion des malheurs dont l'Europe était menacée par l'invaſion de ces nouveaux Vandales; un intérêt profond pour le malheureux Roi de France, & pour toute ſa Famille: mais ils paraiſſaient craindre que le Peuple Anglais ne connût pas aſſez ſes vrais intérêts ; que, délivré du danger pour le moment, il ne ſentît pas aſſez la néceſſité d'en prévenir le retour. Il était une meſure qu'ils n'oſaient conſeiller ; il était un ſentiment qui n'appartenait qu'à l'ame ſeule du Roi. S. M. m'a fait répéter encore tout ce que je ſavais ; & après avoir réfléchi quelque temps, lorſque tout le monde était dans l'attente & le ſilence, Elle m'a dit, *Ecrivez.* J'ai pris la plume, & Elle m'a dicté le Manifeſte que voici.

MANIFESTE.

MANIFESTE.

SA Majeſté Britannique a ſuivi tous les événemens dont la France a été le théâtre depuis quatre ans, avec autant d'attention que d'intérêt, mais en même temps avec un eſprit de juſtice & de modération, dont elle peut prendre l'Europe à témoin.

A l'ouverture des Etats-généraux en 1789, ſa Majeſté, qui s'honore de commander à un peuple libre, & qui, chaque jour, reçoit les preuves les plus touchantes de l'union qui peut exiſter entre la liberté & la fidélité, a vu non-ſeulement ſans envie, mais avec ſatisfaction, que le peuple Français pouvait devenir participant des bénédictions ineſtimables, que répand ſur ſes ſujets une Conſtitution libre, ſage & vigoureuſe, protectrice de tous les individus & conſervatrice de tous les droits.

Des troubles ſe ſont bientôt élevés en France entre l'ancienne autorité, & les autorités naiſſantes : le Roi d'Angleterre n'a pas même voulu ſe ſouvenir de tout ce qui aurait pu le conduire à des réſolutions que la politique ordinaire ſemblait preſcrire, & que la juſtice la plus ſtricte n'aurait pu reprendre. Sa Majeſté s'eſt crue mieux vengée par un oubli généreux que par de ſévères repréſailles. Elle a fait plus : pendant deux ans elle a formé les vœux les plus ardens pour que le

Roi Très-Chrétien, & la Nation Françaiſe, appellée par lui à la Liberté, parvinſſent à s'entendre ſur leurs vrais intérêts, & ſur les moyens d'établir à jamais leur mutuelle & inſéparable proſpérité.

En 1789 on a menacé de brûler les magaſins d'une des premières villes maritimes de France. Sa Majeſté Britannique a témoigné hautement l'horreur qu'elle concevait pour un tel projet; elle a annoncé que les coupables, quels qu'ils fuſſent, ne trouveraient point d'aſyle dans ſes Etats: elle a ſaiſi cette occaſion de renouveller au Roi, & d'exprimer à l'Aſſemblée Nationale de France, des aſſurances de paix & d'amitié, afin que l'un & l'autre, dégagés de toute crainte extérieure, puſſent ſe livrer tout entiers à des travaux d'où dépendait le bonheur de tant de millions d'hommes.

En 1791, la Colonie Françaiſe de Saint-Domingue eſt devenue la proie d'une révolte, & d'une dévaſtation, trop faciles à prévoir; Lord Effingham, d'après les ordres qu'il en avoit reçus de Sa Majeſté, a ſecouru les Colons de vivres & de vaiſſeaux; & des remercîmens publics ont été votés par l'Aſſemblée Nationale de France à Sa Majeſté, & à la Nation Britannique.

Au mois de Septembre de la même année, le Roi Très-Chrétien a fait notifier à Sa Majeſté Britannique, qu'il venait d'accepter la Conſtitution décrétée par l'Aſſemblée Nationale. Sa Majeſté a répondu par l'expreſſion de nouveaux ſouhaits pour le bonheur des parties contractantes, qui venoient de ſe lier l'une à l'autre ſous la foi d'un nouveau ſerment.

Au mois de Juin 1792, la France a déclaré la guerre à l'Empereur. Le Roi Très-Chrétien a fait & réitéré, par ſon Ambaſſadeur, les plus vives inſtances auprès de S. M. B. pour qu'elle perſiſtât dans ſes diſpoſitions amicales, & ne groſsît point le nombre des ennemis de la France: S. M. a été remerciée par le même Ambaſſadeur des *ſentimens d'humanité, de juſtice & de paix, ſi bien manifeſtés dans ſa réponſe*, ainſi que dans *la proclamation royale qu'elle avait publiée en conſéquence.*

Note de M. Chauvelin, 18 Juin 1792.

Sûr des diſpoſitions perſonnelles de S. M., le Roi des Français l'a fait prier *d'employer ſes bons offices*, & même *l'influence de ſa poſition*, pour diminuer le nombre des ennemis de la France, & empêcher qu'*aucune aſſiſtance leur fût donnée, par ſes alliés, directement ou indirectement.* L'Ambaſſadeur Français a fait valoir, à l'appui de cette demande, *l'équilibre de l'Europe, l'indépendance des divers Etats, la paix générale menacée & compromiſe. Sans doute les mêmes ſentimens qui avaient déterminé S. M. B. à ne pas s'immiſcer dans les affaires intérieures de la France, devaient également la porter à reſpecter les droits & l'indépendance des autres ſouverains*; & c'eſt ce qu'elle a poſitivement & franchement déclaré à cette époque;

Ibid.

Note de Lord Grenville, en réponſe à celle de M. Chauvelin, du 18.

mais en même temps, elle a non moins positivement offert l'*intervention* qu'on lui demandait *de ses conseils & de ses bons offices, si elle étoit désirée par toutes les parties intéressées.* En attendant, S. M. se vouait à la plus stricte neutralité; parmi ses alliés, les plus intimes ont embrassé le même systême, & l'ont aussi scrupuleusement observé.

S. M., pénétrée d'affection pour le Roi Très-Chrétien, d'estime pour ses vertus, & d'intérêt pour ses malheurs, n'a pu voir, sans une grande inquiétude, les dangers qu'il avait courus dans la journée du 20 Juin : mais elle a appris en même temps que son courage & sa bonne conscience l'avaient préservé au milieu du péril. Elle a vu bientôt les autorités constituées, les Communes des villes & des campagnes, presque tous les corps administratifs, en un mot, soixante & sept départemens, sur quatre-vingt-trois, environner le Trône de leurs loyales adresses; protester de leur fidélité au Monarque Français; le remercier de sa fermeté, lui offrir leurs cœurs & leurs bras; dévouer à l'infamie & à l'exécration cette journée funeste; solliciter enfin, au nom de la Constitution & de la Nation, la punition de ceux qui avaient, ou médité, ou exécuté, ou toléré cet attentat. Sa Majesté n'a pas été dans la nécessité pénible de sortir de la route qu'elle s'était tracée: elle a, au contraire, pendant quelques instans, espéré, pour la France, le retour de cette tranquillité intérieure, que la paix extérieure eût bientôt suivie.

Malheureusement cet espoir a été de courte durée; de nouveaux germes de discorde ont été semés; leur développement a été aussi rapide, qu'effrayant: les événemens se sont pressés, les désastres se sont multipliés, & l'Europe a vu éclore la journée du 10 Août.

Tout ce qui, le 21 Juin, avait été *la Nation*, ne l'a plus été le 11 Août; & ceux qu'à la première époque on avait appelé *des rebelles*, à la seconde se sont dits le *Gouvernement*. Municipalités, départemens, juges-de-paix, tribunaux, jusqu'à la Constitution; cette constitution qui, vingt-cinq jours auparavant, avait encore été jurée solemnellement, tout a disparu avec le Roi.

Alors S. M. B. a dû rappeler son Ambassadeur; elle l'avait envoyé au Roi des Français, & ce Roi était dans les fers: il ne pouvait résider qu'auprès d'un Gouvernement, & telle chose qu'un Gouvernement n'existait plus en France. Ceux-là même qui, la veille du 10 Août, s'étaient unis pour renverser le Trône, le lendemain s'étaient divisés pour en disputer les dépouilles. Dans cette perpétuelle instabilité entre tous les partis qui, depuis trois ans, déchiraient le Royaume, & qui, selon qu'ils étaient vainqueurs, ou vaincus, s'appelaient tour-à-tour la *Nation*, & la *Faction*, à quel signe S. M. pouvait-elle reconnaître celui qui avait réellement le droit de s'appeler le *peuple Français?*

S. M. a témoigné la douleur profonde dont ſon cœur était affecté par tant de tragiques événemens. Eh ! quel cœur aſſez barbare eût pu s'y montrer inſenſible ? En admettant même qu'on pût balancer entre les deux cauſes, la douleur n'était-elle pas partout ? Chacun n'avait-il pas ſes pertes à déplorer ? Le ſang n'avait-il pas coulé de part & d'autre ? En s'efforçant même de croire que les vaincus avaient été aggreſſeurs, n'y avait-il pas eu un tel abus de la victoire, que les guerres les plus féroces, dans les ſiécles les plus barbares, pouvaient à peine en offrir l'exemple ? La France, frappée dans une de ſes parties, n'était-elle pas menacée dans toutes ? Une Nation également brave & loyale, la Suiſſe entière n'était-elle pas dans le deuil ? Ce deuil n'était-il pas celui de l'Europe ? Craindre & gémir à cette époque, n'était-ce pas s'unir à tous les ſentimens, parler tous les langages ?

A l'expreſſion d'une douleur profonde, Sa Majeſté a réuni le témoignage d'un intérêt preſſant pour le Roi Très-Chrétien, pour ſa Royale Famille, pour leur ſureté, pour leur dignité ; elle a annoncé l'indignation générale qu'exciterait un attentat dont on voudrait les rendre victimes ; elle a fait preſſentir qu'un tel événement ferait néceſſairement violence à ſes diſpoſitions amicales. Qui oſera dire que cette déclaration ne fût pas un devoir pour S. M. ? Quel Roi, quel Peuple, pourvu qu'il ſoit juſte & généreux, peut n'être pas entraîné par le plus vif de tous les intérêts, en voyant tant de probité, tant de courage, tant de vertu, tant de jeunesse, & tant de malheur? Quel homme revêtu d'un pouvoir quelconque, peut ne pas se croire obligé de le déployer tout entier pour prévenir une si horrible injustice? Qu'importe le nombre de ceux qui veulent la commettre? Est-ce pour la force contre la faiblesse, ou pour la faiblesse contre la force, qu'il est beau de s'armer? S. M. B. ne craint pas d'en appeller à tous les cœurs Français; elle est bien sure que, même actuellement, la grande majorité applaudirait à sa déclaration. Si les consciences pouvaient se révéler, elle en appellerait à ceux-là même qui se montrent le plus acharnés à la perte du Roi Très-Chrétien; on verrait que le probe & infortuné Louis XVI n'a peut-être pas un seul ennemi personnel, & que le Roi n'est haï qu'en haine de la Royauté, par ceux qui ont osé la détruire, qui désespèrent de la remplacer, & qui tremblent de la voir renaître.

Mais, même au milieu de ces déclarations éventuelles, S. M. a renouvellé ses assurances de paix; & quand elle a permis que son Ambassadeur vît une fois les dépositaires équivoques d'un Gouvernement provisoire, elle l'a chargé de leur déclarer qu'elle persistait à vouloir observer une entière neutralité entre la France, & les Puissances qu'elle combattait.

Les actions ont été conformes aux discours ; les Français ont joui, dans les Etats de Sa Majesté, de tous les avantages que leur promettaient les traités : tous y ont été reçus, quelles que fussent leurs opinions, & même leurs projets. La sureté, la liberté, la propriété d'aucun n'y a été violée, ni son industrie entravée. Pour le commerce, pour des approvisionnemens en vivres, chevaux, armes, ils ont trouvé toutes les facilités, peut-être trop ; car, parmi les armes, il y en a eu d'un genre plus que suspect. Enfin, jusqu'à ce moment, le Roi n'a encore rien dit, ni rien fait, à l'égard de la France, en quoi il n'ait parlé, ou agi comme un voisin bon, amical, & même indulgent.

Comment a été payé, de la part du Gouvernement Français, cette conduite de S. M. ?

Tant que Louis XVI a été sur le trône, S. M. a reçu de lui le juste retour qu'elle avait droit d'en attendre. Le malheureux Louis XVI aimait à compter sur l'affection de S. M. ; & peut-être s'est-il reproché, plus d'une fois, la guerre aujourd'hui si funeste au Continent Européen, dans laquelle d'imprudens Ministres avaient entraîné sa jeunesse.

Depuis la détention scandaleuse sous laquelle Louis XVI & toute sa famille gémissent depuis quatre mois, il n'est pas d'injure, excepté celle d'une guerre ouverte, qui du moins eût été plus franche, à laquelle le Gouvernement Français ne se soit porté envers S. M.

Son Ambassadeur a été soumis à des refus, à des formes, à une inquisition incompatibles avec le respect dû au caractère de Représentant de S. M.

Ceux de ses sujets qui étaient alors en France, n'ont pas eu la liberté de quitter, quand ils l'ont voulu, une terre où la vie des hommes était livrée à la fureur arbitraire & capricieuse du premier meurtrier, qui souvent même, frappant sans colère & sans objet, se faisait un jeu de l'assassinat.

Il en est qui ont été tenus en chartre privée; il en est qui ont été enlevés la nuit au milieu de leur sommeil, & traînés dans les prisons, lorsque les massacres du 2 Septembre étaient déjà résolus: ils ont réclamé vainement la qualité de sujets de S. M. B.; & ils n'ont dû leur salut qu'au hasard des circonstances.

Deux ont été massacrés.

Des Sociétés entières de Sujets Britanniques ont été obligées, pour se dérober à la mort, d'abandonner des maisons qu'elles possédaient en France, qu'elles y avaient acquises, ou construites, de leurs fonds, & dans lesquelles, sous la protection de S. M. B., sous la sauvegarde des traités, au nom de la liberté de conſcience, proclamée par la France elle-même, elles ſuivaient paiſiblement leurs études, & exerçaient religieuſement leur culte.

Des voyageurs Anglais ont été arrêtés, inſultés, menacés.

Des femmes ont été miſes ſous la garde de fuſiliers, d'autres dépouillées ; il y en a qui ont eſſuyé des outrages pires que la mort.

Des propriétaires qui, aux termes des traités, & même de la Conſtitution Françaiſe, pouvaient poſſéder, acquérir, & contracter en France, ont été rangés parmi ce qu'on appelle les *Emigrés*, parce qu'ils étaient revenus dans leur patrie originelle, & au ſein de leur famille ; leurs biens ont été ſaiſis, leurs revenus pris, & le fonds mis en vente.

Enfin, ces injures partielles, dont quelques-unes tout-au-plus peuvent s'attribuer au haſard, ont été comblées par une injure générale, volontaire & déterminée, la plus ſenſible au cœur de S. M., puiſqu'il s'agit du bonheur de tous ſes ſujets ; la plus criante, puiſque, pour la commettre, il a fallu braver toutes les notions du juſte & de l'injuſte ; violer tout ce qui, depuis l'exiſtence des ſociétés, avait paru ſacré, & renverſer tout ce que la morale & la raiſon univerſelle avaient érigé en loix des nations.

Nobles & fidèles Bretons, c'eſt à vous que S. M. veut adreſſer le récit des ſollicitudes qui ont agité ſon cœur, & des dangers dont il a voulu vous préſerver. Il faut que vous le ſachiez tous : on a formé, on a entrepris, on s'eſt cru au moment de conſommer le projet de mettre toutes nos loix en pièces, d'anéantir cette Conſtitution, ouvrage fortuné de vos glorieux ancêtres, & qui, depuis un ſiècle, vous a élevés au premier rang des plus grandes, comme des plus opulentes Nations.

Ceux qui ont profané leurs temples, blaſphêmé leur Dieu, fait autant de martyrs parmi eux, qu'ils y ont vu d'hommes religieux, ceux-là n'ont pu ſupporter cette élévation & cette pureté d'ame, qui vous font reconnaître, pour premier fondement de votre morale, votre reſpect & vos devoirs envers la Divinité.

Ceux qui ont chargé de fers, d'outrages & de ſupplices un Roi débonnaire, toute ſa Royale Famille, des femmes, des enfans ; ceux-là ſe ſont indignés de l'union qu'ils voient établie entre un peuple ſage, qui chérit un Gouvernement éprouvé ; entre un peuple loyal, qui croit à la ſainteté des ſermens ; entre un peuple bon, qui paie la bienveillance par l'affection ; & un Souverain, qui ne règne que par la loi, qui ne veut être puiſſant que pour vous rendre heureux, qui place ſa grandeur dans votre liberté, & ſon bonheur dans votre amour.

Ceux qui ont violé, incendié, ravi toutes les propriétés, qui ont détruit la ressource du pauvre en dévorant la fortune du riche; qui, après avoir ôté le pain à l'indigent, ont fini par le rendre rare, même pour l'homme aisé; qui ont couvert la France de prisons, de gibets, de ruines, de carnage; ceux-là ont détesté un pays, où le propriétaire, sans méfiance, passe des jours heureux, & des nuits tranquilles; où l'homme industrieux marche à la fortune par la voie de l'honneur; où l'artisan a du travail, & le pauvre, des secours; où la loi seule, & une loi incorruptible, peut priver un homme de sa liberté; où il ne peut être frappé que par le glaive de la justice, qui le frappe encore à regret.

Ceux qui, en ayant sans cesse à la bouche les mots de *liberté* & d'*égalité*, ont introduit l'esclavage le plus insupportable, & la plus monstrueuse inégalité; qui ont puni de mort des opinions, & ont été chercher l'opinion jusques dans le secret des pensées & des écrits; qui ont mis dans la balance de la justice autant de poids différens, qu'ils jugeaient de différentes personnes; qui ont toujours honoré, toujours absous, toujours récompensé les assassins & les brigands; toujours insulté, toujours condamné, toujours immolé les hommes de bien & les propriétaires: ceux qui les premiers ont offert à l'univers le scandale de destituer, d'emprisonner, d'égorger les Juges fidèles à la Loi; ceux qui, en plein tribunal, ont voulu massacrer un *Jury*, parce qu'il venait d'absoudre un accusé; qui ont replongé dans la prison, avec l'aide d'un Juge inique, l'homme qu'une sentence venait de déclarer innocent ; qui ont été chercher un autre *Jury* pour le déclarer coupable, & qui ont trouvé plus simple de le massacrer, sans attendre même le nouveau *Verdict* : ceux-là n'ont pu souffrir qu'il existât près d'eux une Contrée, où la liberté du sujet n'a d'autre borne que celle qui a été posée par la loi, c'est-à-dire, par sa propre volonté ; où l'asyle de la pensée est inviolable ; où l'opinion ne peut se transformer en délit ; où l'erreur est pardonnée, & où il ne peut y avoir de crime que dans les actions. Ils n'ont pu souffrir qu'il existât près d'eux une Contrée où la véritable *égalité* est dans toute sa plénitude, c'est-à-dire, où il n'y a pas un seul homme vivant, s'il est né dans le pays, qui, avec des talens, des vertus, & des services, ne puisse parvenir aux premières places, & atteindre les premiers honneurs ; où le terme d'*homme nouveau* est inconnu ; où la vie, la liberté, la propriété de l'homme le plus obscure sont autant comptées, que celles du personnage le plus éclatant ; où le premier Pair des trois Royaumes, & le plus humble artisan, pèsent autant dans la Balance de la Justice. Ils n'ont pu souffrir qu'il existât près d'eux une Contrée où la Loi est adorée, & où, depuis plusieurs générations, on ignore ce que c'est qu'un juge prévaricateur, un jury corrompu, un magistrat outragé, un accusé indéfendu, & un innocent condamné.

Enfin, ceux qui ont anéanti leur commerce, qui de leurs brillantes colonies ont fait un monceau de cendres détrempées de ſang, qui ont chaſſé une moitié de leur numéraire, qui, n'oſant s'en fier à eux-mêmes, ont enfoui l'autre moitié, qui l'ont remplacé par des papiers frauduleux, par une fauſſe monnoie, que bientôt l'hypothêque de la France entière ne ſuffira peut-être pas à couvrir ; ceux, pour tout dire en un ſeul mot, qui, ſans religion, ſans mœurs, ſans loix, ſans gouvernement, ont détruit, en quatre ans, l'ouvrage de quatorze ſiècles, & ont conduit leur miſérable patrie à l'Anarchie, à la guerre au dedans & au dehors, à la banqueroute & à la famine : ceux-là ont envié & maudit l'ïmmenſité de votre commerce, la proſpérité de vos Colonies, l'amortiſſement de votre dette, la diminution de vos charges, vos tréſors, votre crédit, votre abondance, vos loix, vos vertus.

Sur cette Terre de Juſtice & de Paix, ils ont envoyé un eſſaim d'hommes pervers, chargés d'attirer ſur nous tous les fléaux dont ils avaient accablé leur propre pays : ces hommes ſe ſont diſtribués dans les différentes parties de l'Angleterre, de l'Ecoſſe, de l'Irlande, & juſques dans les Colonies Britanniques. Une hiérarchie ſacrilège a été inſtituée parmi ces apôtres de diſcorde & de crime ; chaque conciliable a connu un chef, qui lui-même en avait pluſieurs ſous lui. Chacun dans ſa proportion, a été largement ſoudoyé, non-ſeulement pour lui, mais encore pour avoir de quoi corrompre ou ſolder les hommes ſimples, paſſionés, méchans, ou criminellement ambitieux, qui dans la Nation la plus ſage, & ſous le Gouvernement le plus juſte, ſont encore trop nombreux. Tous les chefs correſpondaient entre eux ; des émiſſaires allaient ſans ceſſe d'un endroit à l'autre, ſemant des libelles incendiaires, & des exhortations perfides : ils retournaient en France rendre des comptes ; ils revenaient en Angleterre rapportant de nouvelles inſtructions & de nouveaux fonds. Ainſi les adminiſtrateurs actuels de la France, ces hommes qui ont dévoré ſix milliards en trois ans, qui dépenſent 1800 millions dans une année, quoiqu'ils n'en impoſent que 600, & n'en aient perçu, la dernière année, que 187—ces hommes, au lieu de chercher les moyens de procurer quelque paix, & de créer quelque reſſource à leur pays en détreſſe, achevaient de l'épuiſer, & augmentaient encore la misère du peuple Français pour bouleverſer l'Angletere, comme ils avaient bouleverſé la France.

Bretons, regardez autour de vous ; voyez vos maiſons, vos campagnes, vos villes, vos manufactures, vos ports ; parcourez en idée tout l'Empire Britannique ; portez enſuite vos regards ſur la France : comparez ce que vous êtes, & ce qu'on voulait que vous devinſſiez.

S. M. a ſu poſitivement tous ces faits ; elle a connu tous les chefs, les agens, les ſociétés, les correſpondans, les émiſſaires, les époques des conciliabules, des voyages, des réſolutions.

Elle a ſu qui d'entre eux avaient des lettres de crédit indéterminées ; qui d'entre eux étaient payés à tant par mois, par ſemaine, par jour. Elle a ſu que le projet avait été formé de s'emparer de la Tour, de piller l'Arſenal qu'elle renferme, de forcer les priſons, de ſe porter ſur les maiſons des propriétaires, & ſur les offices publics ; en un mot, d'abattre d'un ſeul coup toutes les branches de la Conſtitution. Elle a ſu que l'exécution du projet avait été propoſée pour le Samedi 1er Septembre, ou pour le Lundi 3. Elle a vu le modèle des poignards qui devaient armer les ſéditieux, & qui a été trouvé chez un Français. Elle a ſu où vingt milliers de fer étaient tout préparés pour être façonnés en piques en 36 heures.

Elle a ſu quel membre de la Convention Nationale de France, trouvant les complots trop lents, avait écrit à un des agens, que *ce n'était pas ainſi qu'on travaillait, & qu'il ne gagnait pas l'argent de la république.*

Elle a ſu quels autres membres de la Convention Nationale avaient rédigé un plan pour armer & ſoulever vos Nègres, perdre les Colonies Anglaiſes ; en un mot, pour *bouleverſer l'Angleterre à quelque prix que ce fût.*

Elle a ſu quel émiſſaire, après n'avoir ſéjourné à Londres que 24 heures, était parti pour La Haye, avec la miſſion de *bouleverſer la Hollande.*

Elle

Elle a ſu quel autre émiſſaire a écrit en France vers le milieu de Novembre, promettant que *l'inſurrection allait éclater à Londres*; & a écrit enſuite, vers le milieu de Décembre, *qu'il n'y avait plus d'eſpoir pour l'inſtant*.

Elle a ſu qui, d'entre les chefs, a averti ſes agens que, *la première tentative ayant échoué, il fallait bien prendre garde, avant de ſe déterminer à la ſeconde*.

Elle a ſu le nom & le nombre des canonniers Français qui, ne pouvant plus être employés, en Angleterre, à un complot avorté, ont reçu l'ordre de s'embarquer pour l'Irlande, le Lundi 17 Décembre dernier: elle a ſu quel chef les a contremandés & renvoyés en France, où il eſt retourné lui-même.

Que le Conſeil exécutif proviſoire de France renie l'action du Gouvernement Français dans cette horrible machination, ce n'eſt qu'une équivoque qui ne vaut même pas qu'on s'y arrête. On ſait bien que ce n'eſt pas là qu'eſt la puiſſance; & que ſi quelques membres de ce conſeil ſont individuellement initiés aux myſtères politiques des hommes en pouvoir, collectivement le Conſeil exécutif n'eſt qu'un inſtrument ſervile.

Mais on s'eſt cru tellement ſûr du ſuccès, qu'à Paris on a levé le maſque. Dans la ſéance du 28 Novembre, pluſieurs individus ſe diſant ſujets Britanniques, ont paru à la barre de l'aſſemblée dite

Convention nationale; ils venaient blasphémer la Constitution Britannique: ils annonçaient que, *peut-être dans un tems très-court*, elle n'existerait plus: ils se vantaient d'être rebelles à leur Roi, & à leur Patrie; & la Convention les a couverts d'applaudissemens! Le Président, qui leur a répondu, renchérissant encore sur leur coupable démence, a osé inviter tous les Sujets de la Grande-Bretagne à se révolter contre les Loix de leur Pays, contre le Roi & le Parlement; il a osé dire que la *Royauté était expirante*, & qu'*un feu dévorant allait consumer le Trône*; & de nouveaux applaudissemens se sont fait entendre!

Et cet Acte de Trahison d'une part, cet Acte d'Hostilité de l'autre, il a été décrété que l'impression leur donnerait le caractère le plus solemnel, & la publicité la plus étendue!

Nobles & fidèles Bretons, voilà comment votre Roi a été récompensé de sa Fidélité aux Traités, de la Générosité qui lui a fait dédaigner la Vengeance, de la Modération qui lui a fait refuser la Victoire; du respect qu'il a eu pour le malheur; des vœux qu'il a formés pour le salut des Français: voilà comment vous avez été récompensés de votre intérêt, de votre bon voisinage, de vos Secours, de votre impartiale Hospitalité.

Voilà, en promesses si solemnellement réitérées par l'Ambassadeur Français, voilà *ce respect que le Peuple*

Français devait montrer, dans tous les tems, pour les Loix, les usages, & toutes les formes des Gouvernemens établis dans les pays qui ne l'auraient point attaqué. Voilà ce *désaveu* qu'il prononçait d'avance, cette *sévérité* qu'il s'engageait à exerçer *contre tous ceux de ses agens qui, dans les Cours étrangères & amies, oseraient un seul instant se départir de ce respect, soit en fomentant, soit en favorisant des insurrections contre l'ordre établi, soit en s'immiscant, de quelque manière que ce fût, dans la politique intérieure de ces Etats, sous prétexte d'un prosélitisme qui, exercé envers des Puissances amies, serait une violation réelle des droits des Nations.*

Note officielle, remise par M. Chauvelin, 12 Mai 1792.

Certes si Sa Majesté voulait déployer toutes ses Forces, appeler à Elle, au nom de la Constitution, tous ses fidèles Sujets, & tirer une Vengeance éclatante de tant d'Offenses & de tant de Parjures! jamais Guerre ne fut plus juste, ni plus nationale.

Jamais Guerre, d'un autre côté, ne dût être moins longue, moins dispendieuse, & plus fortunée.

Ce qui reste des Colonies Françaises, fatigué de révoltes, d'incendies, & de massacres, se prosternerait devant le Pavillon Britannique abordant leurs côtes, & leur apportant ce qu'ils ne connaissent plus depuis si long-tems, la paix & des loix.

Les établiſſemens Français tomberaient à la première ſommation faite au nom du Roi de la Grande-Bretagne.

Les Flottes de S. M., rèunies à celles de ſes anciens Alliés (& peut-être il s'en préſenterait de nouveaux) fermant à la fois tous les ports de France, obligeraient le Gouvernement Français de céder enfin à la juſtice, à la raiſon, ſous peine de voir ſa marine s'anéantir, ſes ports s'encombrer, & la famine l'aſſiéger.

Ces Puiſſances coaliſées, auxquelles S. M. avait ſi conſtamment refuſé de ſe joindre, ranimées par une ſi importante diverſion, ſeraient bientôt délivrées de ces armées Françaiſes qui manquent de tout au milieu de leurs brigandages ; de ces armées, auſſi terribles pour le pays qui les a levées, que pour ceux qui les ont reçues, & dont le Gouvernement Français craint encore plus la rentrée, qu'il n'a joui de leurs conquêtes.

Mais S. M. ne ſe croirait pas juſte de voir la Nation Françaiſe dans les factieux par qui elle eſt ou opprimée, ou abuſée ; de voir une Nation juſqu'ici renommée par des vertus brillantes, & des mœurs douces, dans des aſſociations criminelles & féroces, dans un aſſemblage d'hommes ſans aveu & ſans patrie, au milieu deſquels vient ſe refugier quiconque, dans le pays qui l'a vu naître, a encouru le mépris de ſes concitoyens, ou la vindicte des Loix. Il en coûterait au cœur de S. M. de prendre une meſure qui, par le malheur de la néceſſité, envelopperait des innocens dans le ſort des coupables, & ne permettrait pas de diſtinguer, du moins dans les premiers inſtans, ceux qui ont mérité d'être punis, ceux qui doivent encore être plaints, & ceux qui ſont dignes d'être ſecourus, ou qui ont droit à être vengés.

Raſſurée d'ailleurs ſur les dangers preſſans, par le courage & la loyauté de ſes fidèles ſujets, par leur ardeur à ſe rallier autour de la Conſtitution, par les témoignages ſi doux & ſi multipliés de leur attachement à la perſonne du Roi, à ſa Famille, & à ſon Gouvernement ; ſure qu'il n'y a plus rien à craindre, en ce moment, pour la félicité du Peuple Anglais, S M. peut encore eſſayer, avec le Gouvernement Français, la voie de la juſtice & de la modération.

S. M. déclare de nouveau qu'elle veut s'abſtenir de toute intervention dans le gouvernement intérieur de la France. Elle ne prétend pas conteſter à une Nation, le droit de ſe donner des loix. Eh ! plût à Dieu que ce droit eût déjà été exercé dès long-temps ! Qu'il le ſoit enfin ; que dans la France on voie clairement ce qui s'appelle une Nation, & ce qui s'appelle des loix ; & S. M. ne refuſera de contracter avec elle aucun des rapports politiques qui exiſtent entre les différens Peuples de l'Europe.

La France eſt inquiète pour ſes ſubſiſtances, & elle n'a que trop lieu de l'être: S. M. lui offre tous les ſecours qui peuvent dépendre d'elle, & lui permet dans ſes Etats tous les genres de traités & d'approviſionnemens qui n'iront pas au détriment de ſes propres Sujets, à qui elle ſe doit avant tout.

Les Colonies Françaiſes ſont réduites à la ſituation la plus déplorable: S. M. offre au Gouvernement Français, une fois conſtitué, de ſe concerter avec lui pour ramener l'ordre dans ces contrées autrefois ſi proſpères: c'eſt ainſi qu'il convient au Monarque, & au Peuple Anglais, de ſe venger.

La France eſt en guerre avec une moitié de l'Europe; ſes victoires même l'appauvriſſent, & rendent ſon nom odieux; l'Ambaſſadeur Français avait réclamé l'intervention conciliatrice de Sa Majeſté: S. M. répète qu'elle ne refuſera pas ſa médiation, ſi toutes les parties la déſirent.

Mais quand le Roi eſt ſi modéré, il faut qu'on ſoit juſte avec lui: il eſt des conditions que S. M. met à toutes ces offres, & deſquelles il ne lui eſt pas permis de ſe départir.

S. M. dédaigne de demander ſatisfaction, ſoit des émiſſaires qui ſont venus prêcher la ſédition dans ſes Etats, ſoit du Préſident de la Convention Nationale, qui a osé faire, & à la dignité de S. M., & à la loyauté de la Nation Britannique, une insulte sans exemple parmi les Peuples civilisés. Leur punition sera l'impuissance de leurs efforts, & le spectacle si tourmentant pour eux, d'un Roi & d'un Peuple indissolublement unis par une affection réciproque au sein de leur inébranlable Constitution.

Mais l'Ambassadeur Français, *au nom du Peuple Français*, avait donné au Roi l'*assurance formelle que tout ce qui intéressait les droits de* S. M. B., *serait l'objet de l'attention la plus particulière & la plus scrupuleuse*. Les droits de S. M., & ceux de ses Sujets, sont uns ; les premiers n'existent que pour protéger les autres : ces droits ont été & sont journellement violés en France.

L'Ambassadeur Français avait *déclaré* au Roi *que les droits de tous les Alliés de la Grande-Bretagne qui n'auraient point provoqué la France par des démarches hostiles, seraient non moins religieusement respectés*. Les Hollandais ont observé une neutralité aussi scrupuleuse que celle gardée par S. M., & ils sont attaqués dans leurs *droits* les plus positifs par l'ouverture de l'Escaut, & par des manœuvres tramées dans l'intérieur de leur pays.

Note de M. Chauvelin.

L'Ambassadeur Français avait invoqué auprès du Roi *les traités* ; & au mépris de ces traités, qui permettaient aux Sujets des deux Nations d'aller librement d'un royaume à l'autre, même ſans paſſe-port, on a confiſqué les biens, on a proſcrit la tête des Français paiſibles qui voyageaient en Angleterre, comme ſi c'était un crime digne de mort de poſer le pied ſur le ſol Britannique. L'on a trouvé que ce n'était pas encore aſſez, & l'on a été juſqu'à donner à ce Décret, réellement incroyable, un effet rétroactif.

L'Ambaſſadeur Français avait invoqué auprès du Roi, l'*équilibre de l'Europe*, & par-tout cet équilibre eſt détruit; l'*indépendance des divers Etats*, & par-tout cette indépendance eſt violée; *la paix générale menacée, compromiſe*, & c'eſt la guerre générale que le Gouvernement Français déclare à tous les Gouvernemens de l'Europe!

Il avait été proclamé, au nom de la Nation Françaiſe, qu'elle renonçait aux conquêtes: l'Ambaſſadeur Français avait proteſté à S. M. que *quel que fût l'événement de la guerre préſente, la France, religieuſement fidèle à ſa Conſtitution, repouſſait toute idée d'agrandiſſement, & conſerverait ſes limites actuelles.* Cependant des armées Françaiſes ont envahi de toute part le territoire de Puiſſances qui, non-ſeulement n'avaient pas attaqué la France, mais qui même n'avaient pas ſongé à ſe défendre contre elle. Ses limites ont été reculées, & elle a déclaré des régions entières réunies à ſa domination.

Note de M. Chauvelin, 12 Mai 1792.

Il

Il avait été proclamé, au nom de le Nation Française, que le respect des propriétés était la première base de sa nouvelle Constitution. L'Ambassadeur Français assurait que *jamais la France n'avait songé à refuser justice aux Princes d'Allemagne possessionnés sur son territoire.* Cependant le systême de lever des contributions a remplacé celui d'offrir des indemnités: les armées Françaises ont traité, non-seulement les Princes, mais les habitans de Worms, de Mayence, ceux même de Francfort, comme la Légiflature Française traite ceux qu'elle nomme Emigrés. *Ibid.*

Enfin, & c'est-là ce qui importe aujourd'hui, il avait été proclamé, au nom de la Nation Française, que la Personne du Roi était inviolable & sacrée. L'Ambassadeur Français appelait du nom de *pitié outrageante pour le Roi des Français*, l'intérêt qui faisait craindre pour sa personne, & armer pour son salut. Cependant une troupe de parjures & de meurtriers a emprisonné, au nom de la Nation Française, le Roi & toute sa Famille. Ceux qui ont voulu l'assassiner, prétendent le juger !.... D'abord ils l'ont accusé d'avoir conspiré le 10 Août, & d'avoir voulu renverser la Constitution; ensuite ils se sont vantés, à leur tribune, d'avoir été les conspirateurs, d'avoir tramé, entre eux, ce complot du 10 Août: il ont cité les lieux où ils avaient déterminé leur projet, les moyens qu'ils avaient employés pour y parvenir; les décrets par lesquels ils avaient ôté au Roi tous ses défenseurs, ceux par lesquels ils avaient livré l'intérieur de son Palais à la merci des brigands. Ils ont cité une première époque à laquelle leur conjuration avait dû s'exécuter, les raisons qui l'avaient fait différer jusqu'au 10 Août, & l'instant où, dans la nuit, ils avaient fait sonner ce tocsin, funèbre pour tant de milliers d'hommes ; ils ont rivalisé avec acharnement à qui s'attribuerait la plus grande part de cette journée ; & on les a entendu se disputer les uns, à qui avait tramé le plus de complots ; les autres, à qui avait commis le plus d'assassinats. Ils ont avoué que *les hommes du 2 Septembre étaient les mêmes que ceux du 10 Août.* Ils ont avoué que le quatorze Juillet, quand ils renouvelaient solemnellement, à l'autel de la patrie, le *serment de maintenir la Constitution* ; que le 7 Juillet, quand ils juraient de *dévouer à l'exécration les Républicains & les ennemis de la Constitution* ; que le 1er Octobre, c'est-à-dire, dès le premier jour de leur Session, lorsque chacun d'eux, individuellement, montant dans la tribune, &, la main levée vers le Ciel, articulait le serment de *mourir pour cette Constitution*, par laquelle seule ils existaient, *& de la maintenir de tout son pouvoir*, alors ils juraient tous, intérieurement, de renverser cette Constitution. Et voilà qu'oubliant tous ces aveux, ils prétendent encore condamner leur Roi pour avoir conspiré le 10 Août, & avoir voulu renverser la Constitution ! Ils le tiennent pour convaincu ; ils ont enlevé ses papiers sans aucune formalité, pour se laisser le moyen de soustraire, d'ajouter, de falsifier à leur gré ; ils soulèvent ces 48 Sections de la Capitale, qui ne souffrent pas la présence d'un homme de bien, qui, dans la nuit du 10 Août, formaient en tout 492 hommes, & s'intitulaient, *le Peuple Français*. Ils bravent le véritable Peuple, qui, dispersé, désarmé, sans lien, sans organe, & sans chef, pleure en secret le malheur de son Roi, & se sent frappé des mêmes coups que lui.

S. M. B. remet à s'expliquer sur tous les autres griefs qu'elle vient d'indiquer ; elle se borne, dans ce moment, au dernier, le seul pressant, le seul sacré, tant qu'il ne sera pas rempli, le salut du vertueux & infortuné Louis XVI. Elle aime à croire que, même parmi ceux qui gouvernent actuellement son royaume, le plus grand nombre la bénira d'épargner à la Nation Française le plus horrible des parricides, la plus criante des injustices, un désespoir éternel, & une tâche indélébile.

S. M. déclare donc, soit au Conseil Exécutif Provisoire, soit à la Convention Nationale, en un mot, à tout Corps, & à tout individu, dans lequel repose, en France, le pouvoir, que la première condition que le Roi d'Angleterre, & la Nation Britannique, mettent à l'oubli des offenses qui leur ont été faites, c'est que le Roi Louis XVI, la Reine son épouse, & toute sa Royale Famille, soient mis en liberté, & conduits jusqu'au port, où une escadre de S. M. B. les recevra, pour les transporter dans l'asyle qu'une Nation généreuse & hospitalière s'honorera de leur offrir.

Déclarant S. M. que, ſi aucun attentat était commis contre aucun membre de cette Famille, bien plus ſacrée encore par ſes vertus & par ſes malheurs, que par ſa dignité ; alors S. M. jure, à la face du Ciel, qui protégera une cauſe ſi ſainte, de ſe joindre, avec toutes ſes forces, à toutes les parties qui ſeront intéreſſées à tirer vengeance d'un ſi exécrable forfait. S. M. jure de déployer, avec elles, tout ſon pouvoir pour aider la France aſſervie, à ſe délivrer du joug ſanglant que lui impoſent des factieux déſavoués & déteſtés par la grande majorité de la véritable Nation Françaiſe. S. M. jure enfin d'être la première à provoquer le concert de toutes les Puiſſances, pour qu'aucun aſyle ſur la terre ne ſoit accordé à ces meurtriers des Peuples & des Rois, qui auront mérité d'être proſcrits par le genre-humain.

IN WHICH THE CONDUCT OF

MR. LENOX, AND THE MINISTER,

IN THE AFFAIR WITH HIS ROYAL HIGHNESS

THE DUKE OF YORK,

IS FULLY CONSIDERED.

BY THEOPHILUS SWIFT, ESQ.

The King covered his Face; and the King cried with a loud Voice, O my Son! ii. Sam. xix. 24.

THE FOURTH EDITION.

LONDON:

PRINTED FOR JAMES RIDGWAY, YORK-STREET, ST. JAMES'S-SQUARE.

MDCCLXXXIX.

TO THE KING.

SIR,

AN individual who has both the happineſs and the honour to be perſonally known to Your Majeſty, begs permiſſion to approach Your throne, and to lay before You his ſentiments of a late public tranſaction, thro' which the dignity of Your crown has been invaded, and the ſafety of Your people alarmed and endangered.

I ſhould not, however, have preſumed to addreſs my Sovereign on a ſubject of ſuch magnitude and importance, had others of more conſequence than myſelf, and of more ability to execute the very arduous undertaking, come perſonally forward on an occaſion ſo preſſing and intereſting to the empire. Much as I reſpect and love the whole Houſe of Brunſwick;—much as I regard the rights of ſucceſſion, and the ſacred images that reflect Your Royal Perſon; — much as I revere the blood that, deſcending from the pureſt founts of Glory and Virtue, rolls hereditary in the veins of Your illuſtrious offspring;—it is poſſible I might not have engaged in ſo painful a taſk, had not the conduct of Your Majeſty's miniſter excited a ſuſpicion of an alarming nature. The nation, with equal horror and amazement, have beheld an attempt made by an illegitimate

illegitimate defcendant of the Stuart family, to cut off the lawful iffue and prefumptive heir of Your crown*. Had the attempt been rafhly hazarded by a hot-headed young man, who had conceived his own polluted perfon infulted by Royalty, pity for his weaknefs had perhaps ftifled the ftronger emotions of contempt or indignation. But when feveral days had elapfed between the fuppofed affront and the execution of vengeance, by a deliberate attack on the life of Your Second Son, to what impulfe, to what motive, fhall we impute fuch extraordinary conduct?— To fay that Mr. Lenox was ftimulated by the feelings of honour, were

* Perhaps more properly defignated "Pre-"fumptive Heir to the Heir Apparent."

an affront to the dignity of Human Nature; an affront to truth; an affront to every officer that bears Your Majeſty's commiſſion. Men of warm and nice feelings reſent on the ſpot: the voice of honour is a call ſuperior to delay: Offended Virtue is an importunate creditor; ſhe *draws* at ſight, and will be paid on demand. The claims of nature are ſtrong; they *will* be ſatisfied; and the laws of the country, which, philoſophically ſpeaking, are devoid of paſſion, wiſely make allowance for the impulſe of the moment. Men of honour are not apt to *plan* away the lives of others, much leſs of the Princes of the empire, whereof they themſelves are ſubjects. They conſult not whiſperers; neither run they up and

down

down in corners and club-rooms to acquire proof of imaginary provocations. They are governed by no ſuch procraſtinated reſentments, ſuch illiberal ideas, ſuch narrow notions of honour! To what motive then ſhall we aſcribe the conduct of that man who hath diſcovered ſo ſmall a portion of thoſe *fine ſenſations* by which men of dignified and exalted feelings are influenced? Shall we impute it to the blood that runs polluted in his veins? or to the cabals of ſome other perſon? To one, or to the other of theſe, his conduct muſt finally be referred. If to the firſt, then is Mr. Lenox beneath the reſentment of thoſe whoſe generous birth ranks them in the claſs of gentlemen. If to the latter, on whom is it natural that

that we ſhould turn our eyes? On a ſtranger? or on the man who had ſo recently attempted to cramp and cripple, by a moſt dangerous, moſt unprecedented, and moſt unconſtitutional Bill of Regency, the immediate Succeſſor and Repreſentative of Your Majeſty? If it ſhall appear that ſuch man hath uniformly inſulted the Princes of Your houſe;--if he hath been obſerved, at the very inſtant that the iron of Mr. Lenox's rage flamed the hotteſt, to walk in amity and familiarity with the very man who had meditated the deſtruction of his Prince;—ſhall it be ſaid that his conduct does not juſtify ſuſpicion? or that injuſtice is done to him by preſuming him the guilty ſuggeſter of the deed? Shall not a deluded people take the alarm? Shall their

juſt

juſt ſuſpicions be lulled into a dangerous ſecurity? Shall they paſſively endure the inſult? Shall they ſilently behold their Prince degraded, and his life expoſed to the revenge of an imperious ambition?—to that haughty hatred of your crown and family which has ſyſtematically marked the conduct of Your miniſter? As a father, Your Majeſty muſt ever bleed for the dark and daring attempt that has been made on the life of a deſervedly beloved child, not more the darling of Your heart, than the mirror of Your own diſtinguiſhed greatneſs. As the father of Your people, You muſt lament, with them, the vengeance employed againſt an excellent and amiable youth, to whom the nation looked up with equal joy and reverence;

ence; and whoſe ſacred perſon even foreigners regard with eſteem: for Your Majeſty does not require to be told, that all Europe, at this moment, ſtands aſtoniſhed at the deed, and can ſcarcely credit the unreſented violence that has been offered to Your Houſe.

The conduct of the Royal Duke has excited the admiration of every court in Europe. His Majeſty of Pruſſia, when the report of the Prince's magnanimity reached his ear, exclaimed in a rapture, "Were my "uncle living, how would the vete-"ran rejoice to find that his pupil "had acted up to his inſtructions!" If ſuch were, and ſuch undoubtedly *was*, the language of the Pruſſian Monarch, with what contempt, with what

what indignation, with what horror muſt he behold the conduct of Mr. Lenox—of *that man* whom Your miniſter has had the addreſs to convert from a Coward to a Hero;—from a Bravo to a Soldier of Honour? But, alas! England is the only country in which Mr. Lenox is reputed a hero.

Sir, for myſelf, I am neither aſhamed nor afraid to ſay, that I love my king, and regard all the branches of his houſe. My anceſtors loſt much of their blood, and much of their fortunes in the Royal ſervice. I am not a boaſtful man; but ſhould their deſcendant be called on, it is poſſible he might not ſhrink from his duty, or diſhonour his birth. Sure I am, he would defend with his blood the life of the excellent youth which has been wantonly, and I will add, moſt deliberately endangered. I truſt, therefore, that howſoever feebly the preſent queſtion may be argued by me, I ſhall at leaſt obtain credit for my zeal and ſincerity in defence of the honour of Your houſe, the ſafety of Your throne, and the dignity of the country at large. Under this ſanction, I have ventured to throw myſelf at the feet of Your Majeſty, and to claim Your indulgence, whilſt I expreſs the emotions of a loyal and bleeding heart. It is a duty which I owe to my Prince; and, in the diſcharge of that duty, I feel myſelf confidently right. Forward, however, I have not been found on the preſent occaſion: hoping the ſanguinary ſcene at Wimbledon would have been

been confined to the ſpot, and that it would never have penetrated behind the royal curtain;—dear as I deemed the life and intereſts of the Prince, I delayed to draw my pen until other nations had taken the alarm, and publicly expreſſed their fears and aſtoniſhment. Theſe, I truſt, will be found ſufficient motives both for my having continued ſilent ſo long, and for my being the only man who has, even thus late, *perſonally* met the queſtion.

But if, as a *ſubject*, (and it is my boaſt, Sir, that I am Your's,) I deplore and ſhudder at the deſperate attempt, what muſt be the ſufferings of an injured and inſulted Monarch, whoſe parental feelings do honour, not leſs to Royalty than to Human

Nature itſelf?—Of Him, whoſe affection for the children of his loins is the theme of thouſands, and an example to all mankind? It is not for me to paint the diſtreſſes of a wounded monarch, and afflicted father; but allow me to ſay, that my heart rains tears whilſt I but think of it.

On the Beloved Partner of Your griefs and pleaſures, with unaffected concern I would turn my eyes: on Her, to whoſe ſoftneſs of ſoul, whoſe mildneſs of heart, whoſe parental affection the whole nation has borne ample teſtimony. How vaſt then, and ſevere, how deep and ſearching the diſtractions which tear and rend the boſom of that amiable woman! To vent them aloud in ſighs, or diſcharge them in tears, is the privilege

of

of the meaneſt ſubject; yet this, it ſeems, is denied unto Her; and her maternal feelings are publicly ſacrificed on the altar of *State-Policy*, to gratify the inordinate ambition and inſulting pride of a young, imperious miniſter. The very *Sanctum* of Your palace has been violated, and the ſenſibility of a wounded mother unnaturally ſported with, to give colour to the deed.

Pregnant, however, with alarm and horror, as this inſtance of your miniſter's conduct appears to the nation, a more dreadful danger lurks in the back-ground. From his ſtudied irreverence towards all the branches of Your Royal Houſe, what may not be preſumed? I am not a man diſpoſed to anticipate evil, or indulge ſuſpicion; but God forbid that any

man,

man, misled by a false ambition, should assume a parity with Your royal offspring; or should start up in any shape, or under any pretence, the rival of their claims! Human Nature, I trust, is not wholly capable of such insidious depravity: but should the several branches of the Brunswick house be lopped off one by one ——

I beg leave to state a fair proposition; and I implore Your Majesty's gracious attention:—That, had Your illustrious house consisted of two branches only; and if, by any conspiracy, one of them had been cut off, it remained with Heaven alone to say where the national confusion and calamity would have ended! but ever praised be the King of Kings, who hath guarded Your throne with a thick ſhade of ſurrounding branch-es; which neither the lightning of a mortal arm can pierce, nor the thun-der of diſloyalty deſtroy.

But though a man ſhould be found who might lop the branch, it were yet impoſſible to root the ſtock out of the heart of every Engliſhman! For one, I can tell him, that it is deeply planted *there:* and I hope to hear this expreſſion echoed from Eng-land, from Ireland, and from the re-moteſt ſkirts of the Britiſh empire.

But it may be aſked, could a cold and cautious miniſter all at once throw of the maſk, and openly em-brace the man who had fired at the ſon of his royal maſter? The queſtion ſurpriſes, but the anſwer is ſtill more aſtoniſhing. By ſuch *unuſual* conduct

he

he invited the nation to look upon him: the door of perſonal protection flew open; the aſylum of office preſented itſelf to the miniſters of faction, impatient to thin the number of thoſe that ſtood in the way of his ambition. This is the anſwer that muſt be given to it:—let Corruption find another, if ſhe can.

I ſhall not here draw a picture of the hated Houſe of Stuart, and its deteſted adherents; neither ſhall I enlarge on the virtues and the glories that follow the illuſtrious line of Brunſwick. Compariſon would only enflame, and a parallel render that odious which was meant to be merely juſt. This, however, muſt not be paſſed by without particular attention; That if the bar of baſtardy

caſt

caſt between Mr. Lenox and Your Son, be of no conſideration in the queſtion, (as Your miniſter, and his friends, affect to ſay) then is the competitor of Your Son one degree nearer to the Throne of theſe kingdoms than the Prince. Reſpect, Sir, forbids me to ſay more; and I draw a curtain over the offenſive picture.

On the other hand, ſhould it be urged that the bar of illegitimacy *does* ſtand acroſs the eſcutcheon of this proud young man, and therefore that the apprehended danger doth not apply, this concluſion naturally flows from it; that the perſon of Mr. Lenox requires that purity which conſtitutes the gentleman, by rendering him an object deſerving a competition with thoſe who boaſt an unpolluted deſcent; and therefore, not having the purity in himſelf, that he condeſcended to become the inſtrument of another.

Let us not be told that Your Majeſty purified his blood, and made Mr. Lenox a gentleman, the day you made him an officer, and gave him a commiſſion to guard and defend Your own ſacred perſon. This argument, however, will hardly be urged; for the conduct of Mr. Lenox were but the more culpable on that very account. Thus, which ever way the queſtion is turned, the advocates for Mr. Lenox are foiled and defeated.

Had the Royal Duke fallen by the hand of a Ruſſell or a Howard, (dreadful as the thought muſt ever be!) it had not been ſo lamentable. Poſterity

rity might ſay, that the gallant youth had greatly died, as he greatly lived. Had he fallen even by the legitimate houſe of Stuart, no diſhonour had attended his fall;—ſome portion of the old Britiſh honour had revived amongſt us, to conſole us for the irreparable loſs of his much-valued life; —to awaken in our boſoms the virtuous flames that had ſlept ſo long!

But, for a moment, I will ſuppoſe, with Your miniſter, that the feelings of Mr. Lenox were ſtung by ſomething the Prince had ſaid either *to* him, or *of* him. The queſtion will then ſtand thus: Not whether Mr. Lenox had a right to challenge the gentleman, who, he conceived, had offended him? But, WHETHER HE HAD ANY RIGHT AT ALL TO FIRE AT THE

PRESUMPTIVE HEIR OF THE CROWN? This ſimplifies the queſtion, and it does not require much labour of argument to determine the point. For my own part I am free to ſay, at the hazard of my legal reputation, that to *challenge*, or to *fire at* the preſumptive heir of the crôwn, are acts beyond thoſe of a ſimple miſdemeanour; and that if they be not high treaſon, they approach to ſomething extremely like it. When a Prince is born to us, the legiſlature always adaddreſs the throne on the joyous occaſion; juſtly obſerving, that ſuch birth is a freſh acceſſion of ſecurity to the empire. In like manner, whenever the viſitation of God ſnatches from the world a Prince of the realm, an addreſs of condolence waits upon the throne,

throne, commemorating a circumſtance ſo unfortunate to the country. For the ſame reaſon, and to preſerve the rights of ſucceſſion inviolate, the life of a Prince of Wales is wiſely hedged round with ſtatutes; — the ſhade of thoſe ſtatutes covers and extends over the heir preſumptive, as the ſword of the Angel turned every way to guard the tree of life. But even Paradiſe has ceaſed to be ſecure from pollution; nor is the hereditary tree of monarchy always ſafe from the unhallowed hand of violence.

I am no friend to the multiplication of penal ſtatutes; but as a profeſſor of the laws, and an aſſertor of the rights and ſecurity of the throne, I feel myſelf more immediately called

on

on to ſuggeſt the neceſſity of a ſolemn act of the whole legiſlature to protect the lives and perſons of the ſeveral Princes of the Royal Blood. When the Scythian philoſopher * objected to Solon,

* *Anacharſis.* This philoſopher is, perhaps, the ſtrongeſt inſtance on record of the uncultivated powers of the human mind. Born and living in a barbarous, uncivilized country, ſo vaſt were the depths of his wiſdom, and ſo wide the extent of his reputation, that the celebrated Solon travelled into Scythia on purpoſe to conſult him on the framing of the laws, which he afterwards eſtabliſhed at Athens; and which, no doubt, derived conſiderable advantage from the advice of Anacharſis. It was at this famous interview that the Scythian Sage delivered that memorable ſaying, which has ſince been retailed, without acknowledgment, for more than two thouſand years. It is time, however, that it ſhould be reſtored to its original author, though Valerius Maximus has been

Solon, that his code of laws had not provided againſt the crime of *parricide*, the law-giver of Athens anſwered, " That crime is impoſſible." Experience, however, proved this famous

been beforehand with me: " Quam porro ſubtili-" ter Anacharſis leges Arancarum telis compa-" rabat." De Sap. Dict.

The good and learned Prieſt of Apollo thus commemorates the ſaying:—

Γραμμασιν—ἁ μηδεν των αραχνιων διαφερειν, αλλ' ως εκεινα, τȣς μεν ασθενεις και λεπτȣς των αλισκομενων καθεξειν υπο δε των δυνατων και πλȣσιων διαρραγησεσθαι. Plut. Vit. Sol.

Which may be thus put into an Engliſh dreſs. ſhould a tranſlation, at the very moment I am writing, be allowed me.

Like that illuſive net Arachne draws,
To catch the weak, are fram'd the ſubtle laws;
The rich, the mighty break the cobweb through:—
'Twas Anacharſis firſt pronounc'd it true.

legiſ-

legiſlator to be miſtaken; for, not long after, it was found expedient to enact an expreſs law againſt this *impoſſible crime.* A late event has demonſtrated, that the laws of Great Britain have not yet provided againſt every poſſible ſpecies of *parricide*; thus evincing the neceſſity of an immediate and irrevocable act of parliament, rendering it high treaſon for any perſon to conſpire or compaſs the death of a Prince of the empire. Were an act to guard Your children and all future Princes of the country from conſpiracies or violence recommended from the throne, Your loyal people, with one heart and one voice, would ſpring to meet the wiſhes of Your Majeſty; and I will venture to ſay, without fear of contradiction, there

there would not be found a duelliſt in the kingdom hardy enough to oppoſe it.

The more the conduct of Mr. Lenox is conſidered, the more planned and premeditated the whole of it appears. His firſt attack is made on the elder brother of the Royal Duke, who, he well knew, was conſtitutionally prevented from reſenting the inſult. This ſingle circumſtance marks, by the way, that ſort of ſpirit which actuated Mr. Lenox. But this is not all: he inſults the Heir Apparent of the crown, with toaſting in his teeth a name deſervedly odious and offenſive to his Royal Highneſs;—a name that had ſown the ſeeds of family diſſention in the very boſom of the Court;—a name that the Prince himſelf, it is confidently ſaid, had ironically thanked for thoſe diſſentions;—a name that had queſtioned the Prince's natural right of Regency;—a name that had falſely villified the virtue, and traduced the honour of that high and moſt illuſtrious character;—a name on theſe, as well as on other accounts, which Mr. Lenox *well knew* that his Prince deteſted. Here then we behold Your Majeſty's miniſter become the very founder and conductor of the tragedy; he appears in the firſt act; then ſtands behind the curtain; now prompts the actor; now manages the puppet: and were any thing wanting to complete the unfolding of the plot, he appears again, in his own proper perſon, in the very laſt ſcene.

It

It is not fair to judge of a man's conduct by detached parts. Consistence, and an apt concurrence of circumstances, are the proper guides to ascertain the truth of a complicate fact. Thus, had not some one of Your Majesty's family been marked for destruction, the sickle of Mr. Lenox's courage might have reaped its full harvest of satisfaction in that field of honour to which others were anxious to attend him. The members of D'Aubigny's Club, almost to a man, flamed with resentment, and stood on tiptoe with their swords, in defence of their insulted Prince. But this did not suit the purpose of Mr. Lenox; he must have Royal Blood, or none: and since he could not challenge the Heir Apparent of the

Crown without incurring a præmunire, the Heir Preſumptive muſt be made the ſacrifice! This, Great Sir, is the man, for whom Your miniſter gathers laurels, as a proof of his attachment to the Houſe of Brunſwick!

For my own part, I feel no difficulty in declaring, that Mr. Lenox does not appear to me to be a hero. If his courage required ſatisfaction, it ſtill continues unſatisfied; for to ſhoot at another, is no mark of perſonal valour. Had the Prince returned his fire, his honour might poſſibly be ſaid to receive ſatisfaction from that circumſtance; but at preſent, his courage ſtands preciſely in the ſame ſituation that it ſtood in *before he fired at Your Son*. A deciſion indeed of his brother-officers has

has given this matter a different turn, and therefore it does not become me to queſtion it; but a rumor prevails, and it is generally ſuppoſed to be founded in truth, that His Highneſs, with that greatneſs of ſoul which ſhould diſtinguiſh princes, and which always characteriſes the brave, requeſted the officers of the regiment to make a favourable report of Mr. Lenox. A requeſt coming from ſuch a quarter was met, no doubt, half-way, by the lenity and generoſity of thoſe to whom it was directed; and I honour the gentlemen for the determination which they came to.— Should the fact be true, and, from all the circumſtances of the caſe, there is no reaſon to diſbelieve it, the amiable humanity of the Duke ſhines as diſtinguiſhed *out* of the field, as his

magnanimity

magnanimity *in* it was conſpicuous. If, however, the ſentence on Mr. Lenox aroſe from the uncourted opinion of his brother-officers, the *neceſſity* of his quitting the regiment does not ſtrike me. To relinquiſh the good opinion of his own officers, in order to ſeek it among others, with whom, it is poſſible, he might not find it, were inconſiſtent with that *deliberation* which Mr. Lenox appears to have uſed in every other part of the buſineſs.

Every ſubject of the Britiſh empire has virtually ſworn allegiance to the Houſe of Brunſwick. An attempt therefore to deſtroy any part of it, is a breach of that civil obligation by which the ſeveral members of the ſtate are bound to Your Majeſty.—The lifted arm of violence, levelling deſtruction

deſtruction at one of Your children, is a picture the moſt awful that human imagination can form!—A civic wreath was decreed to the Roman who had ſaved the life of a common citizen: but with Us, CHRISTIANS and BRITONS, the deſtruction of a prince, in the opinion of the very miniſters of the country, merits an ovation! I would, however, aſk this plain and obvious queſtion;—which diſcovered the greater magnanimity and the greater patriotiſm, the Prince, who preſerved the life of a ſubject? Or, the Subject that would have taken away the life of his Prince? There is no ſubtilty, no ambiguity in the queſtion: liſping ſimplicity might anſwer it.

The coolneſs, not leſs than the

courage

courage of the Prince, is a theme of damiration to every thinking mind. But coolneſs is always the attendant on true courage, as mercy and meekneſs are its inſeparable companions. This the gallant Duke manifeſted in an eminent degree. *He preſerved the life of a citizen*, at the ſame time that he expoſed his own to a raſh intemperate man. By his conduct he has taught the world this admirable leſſon, That to take away the life of another, is an offence againſt Him who originally gave it ;—an offence againſt the ſtate from which we derive protection. That a Prince, like Him who delegates his power to his images on earth, ſhould have more delight in *ſparing* than *deſtroying* ; and that pardon is the privilege of greatneſs.

greatneſs. Above all, his moderation has ſecured the lives of all future Princes in this country. No man, who is not content to paſs for what he would not be thought, can hereafter challenge his Prince. The example of the great is prevalent, and that of Kings and Princes more generally extenſive. When Harry IV. of France had publiſhed an arret againſt duelling, within the ſpace of twenty-four hours he defeated the very object of that edict. On his journey to Fontainbleau, obſerving a ſoldier that had fallen in a duel, the native ardour of his ſoul broke out with an involuntary impulſe in the following indiſcreet exclamation,—"That man lies in the bed of honour!" The expreſſion was in-

F ſtantly

ſtantly echoed through the kingdom, and was urged, upon all affairs of honour, as the firſt and laſt excuſe for duelling. So vaſt is the influence of a great authority! But the more glorious, becauſe the more virtuous Prince of theſe days, has, by his great example, checked the falſe ardor that has gone abroad, without diminiſhing the luſtre of his own heroic ſpirit. Virtue is true dignity; and never appears to more advantage than when ſhe waits on Princes.

But, for a moment, let us ſuppoſe, that the Prince had actually fired at this hot young man. What a crowd of ſerious reflections riſe before us and occupy our minds, whilſt we but barely fancy the picture! What?— a Prince ſet ſo dreadful an example

to

to pofterity ?—a Prince defcend from his dignity, to indulge the pride, by fhedding the blood of a contaminated rival ?—a Prince degrade himfelf to an equality with a man fo vaftly his inferior in the race of glory ?—When Alexander was challenged to run at the Olympic Games, he made this great reply; "I would accept "the offer, were kings my competi-"tors!" The loftinefs of the anfwer proved the dignity of the mind that delivered it; and I give it in *Englifh*, that every *Englifhman* may underftand it.

The next picture, though much too flattering to pafs for real, is, "Mr. Lenox fufpending the rage of "his arm, and waiting the fire of his "Prince." A more beautiful picture cannot well be imagined. Great minds may conceive it, and heros perhaps believe it. It was reserved for Mr. Lenox and the Minister to reverse the tapestry.

Having detained Your Majesty so long, I shall not stop to enlarge on the conduct of Lord Winchelsea, who, like Mr. Lenox, does not appear to me to be a hero, or to have consulted either the safety of Your House, or the dignity of Your Throne. As a domestic attendant on the person of Your Majesty, it was his strong and indispensable duty to have defended Your palace from violence. As an hereditary counsellor of the Crown, he should not have advised or abetted the destruction of any part of it. Robed in the scarlet of honour, he should

ſhould not have tarniſhed its luſtre, or dipped in the dye of faction, by becoming the *Second of the Second* in a tranſaction that has brought ſuch diſgrace upon the country.

Here, Sir, allow me to cloſe the unhappy ſcene. An affectionate and loyal ſubject, than whom You have not in your dominions one that loves You better, or that reſpects You more, beſeeches You to pardon the freedom that his zeal has prompted him to uſe with his Sovereign. He begs leave to aſſure Your Majeſty, that he has had no adviſers whatever on the ſubject of the preſent Letter; that he has conſulted nothing but his own feelings, the ſafety of Your Throne, and the dignity of Your people; that his faults and offences are all his own; and that, let his political

opinions

opinions be what they may, his respect and regard for the Perfon of Your Majefty have always continued inviolate. If he has fpoken difrefpectfully of Your minifter, it did not arife from any difaffection for Your Majefty. He thought Your fervant had not done his duty; for it was his duty, as a ftatefman, to have known, that the life of Your Son was in danger; and, knowing it, it was equally his duty to have ftept in, and prevented it.

I truft, Sir, that, on a former occafion, when I had the high honour to addrefs You, the effufions of my loyalty evinced a heart glowing with zeal for Your Perfon, and attachment to Your Throne. Time has not abated the fervor of my affection

tion, or weakened the impreſſions of my duty. Your Majeſty's gracious reception of my unaſſuming, but loyal, offering, can never be blotted from my memory: and I am too conſcious of the ſincerity of my own heart, to doubt or queſtion the greatneſs of my Sovereign's. But though I were capable of forgetting my fealty, I muſt always remember the dignity I owe to myſelf;—a dignity that, whilſt it impels me to deliver my ſentiments with freedom, ſecures me from offering the leaſt intended inſult to Majeſty.

To You, Royal Sir, as the great fountain of honour, I have ventured to ſubmit this ſolemn appeal on a point of *honour* the moſt momentous that ever employed the pen of an author,

thor, or engaged the attention of a great nation. As a private individual, I feel myſelf proud in the honour I have aſſumed of writing to my King; —to a Monarch, for who mmy eſteem is not leſs than my affection. Having aſpired to this high conſequence, I ſhall not condeſcend to make the leaſt reply to any anſwer which may come from an inferior quarter.

That Your Majeſty may long enjoy an uninterrupted ſtate of health and glory, of happineſs and ſafety, is the fervent prayer of Your Majeſty's moſt loyal,

moſt dutiful,

and moſt affectionate ſubject,

THEOPHILUS SWIFT.

Wigmore-ſtreet, June 25, 1789.

F I N I S.

www.ingramcontent.com/pod-product-compliance
Lightning Source LLC
Chambersburg PA
CBHW021106270326
41929CB00009B/747

* 9 7 8 3 3 3 7 2 9 7 5 1 0 *